RECLAIM

a Generation

(VOLUME 2)

21 DAYS OF PRAYER FOR SCHOOLS

CHERYL SACKS

BRIDGEBUILDERS
INT'L LEADERSHIP NETWORK

PRAYERSHOP
PUBLISHING

Terre Haute, Indiana

PrayerShop Publishing is the publishing arm of the Church Prayer Leaders Network. The Church Prayer Leaders Network exists to equip and inspire local churches and their prayer leaders in their desire to disciple their people in prayer and to become a "house of prayer for all nations." Its online store, prayershop.org, has more than 150 prayer resources available for purchase or download.

ISBN (Print): 978-1-970176-25-4

ISBN (E-Book): 978-1-970176-26-1

Scripture quotations marked (AMPC) are taken from the Amplified® Bible Classic Version. Copyright © 1954, 1958, 1962, 1964, 1965, 1987 by The Lockman Foundation. Used by permission. www.lockman.org

Scripture quotations marked (ASV) are taken from the American Standard Version of the Bible. Public Domain.

Scripture quotations marked (ESV) are from the ESV® Bible (The Holy Bible, English Standard Version®), Copyright © 2001 by Crossway, a publishing ministry of Good News Publishers. Used by permission. All rights reserved.

Scripture quotations marked (KJV) are taken from the King James Bible. Public Domain.

Scripture quotations marked (MSG) are taken from *THE MESSAGE*, Copyright © 1993, 2002, 2018 by Eugene H. Peterson. Used by permission of NavPress. All rights reserved. Represented by Tyndale House Publishers, a Division of Tyndale House Ministries.

Scripture quotations marked (NIV) are taken from the Holy Bible, New International Version®, NIV®. Copyright © 1973, 1978, 1984, 2011 by Biblica, Inc.™ Used by permission of Zondervan. All rights reserved worldwide. www.zondervan.com. The "NIV" and "New International Version" are trademarks registered in the United States Patent and Trademark Office by Biblica, Inc.™

Scripture quotations marked (NLT) are taken from the Holy Bible, New Living Translation, Copyright ©1996, 2004, 2015 by Tyndale House Foundation. Used by permission of Tyndale House Publishers, a Division of Tyndale House Ministries, Carol Stream, Illinois 60188. All rights reserved.

Scripture quotations marked (PHILLIPS) are taken from The New Testament in Modern English, copyright © 1958, 1959, 1960 J.B. Phillips and 1947, 1952, 1955, 1957 The Macmillan Company, New York. Used by permission. All rights reserved.

Scripture quotations marked (TPT) are from The Passion Translation®. Copyright © 2017, 2018 by Passion & Fire Ministries, Inc. Used by permission. All rights reserved. ThePassionTranslation.com

TABLE OF CONTENTS

WEEK 3: Ignite Spiritual Awakening on Campuses | 69

APPENDIX

INTRODUCTION:
THE WAR OVER OUR CHILDREN

"If the foundations are destroyed, what can the righteous do?"
(PSALM 11:3, ESV)

*"For the weapons of our warfare are not of the flesh but have
divine power to destroy strongholds. We destroy arguments
and every lofty opinion raised against the knowledge of
God, and take every thought captive to obey Christ."*
(2 CORINTHIANS 10:4-5, ESV)

Perhaps, like me, you are deeply concerned about what you see happening in schools around our nation. You've picked up this book because you want to know how to pray and what you can do. You want to make a difference.

The truth is that no matter what we see with our natural eyes, we can be confident the Lord has a great plan for this young generation! At the same time, as we can very clearly see, Satan has declared war, strategizing how he can steal, kill, and destroy them (see John 10:10). To this end, he has managed to infiltrate every sphere of culture—including media and entertainment, business, government, science and technology, and, *yes*, even education—with an agenda to take down the family and destroy our children. He is strategically working on a coordinated, destructive plan—and our children are the target.

This agenda is accelerating before our very eyes, and it's clear that the goal is to capture the hearts and minds of the next generation.

Currently, the foundations of our education system—and its children—are under moral and intellectual assault like never before. Fewer and fewer Americans believe in a clear and distinct right or wrong, and often our public schools are reinforcing these new norms as "progressive," "just," and "inclusive."

In recent decades, we've seen educational standards diminished, prayer in schools abolished, the Word of God removed, socialist and radical sex education introduced, and anti-Christ and anti-Christian curricula implemented. Some elementary schools have gone so far as to approve after-school Satan clubs sponsored by The Satanic Temple. All-out war has been waged against our children's spiritual, mental, and emotional growth as well as their sexual identity.

To be certain, we did not get to this precipice overnight. Nevertheless, it is not too late for Christians to awaken from our slumber and realize that we are in a pitched battle with forces beyond our comprehension—and at stake are the precious, eternal lives of our own children and grandchildren. This battle for the next generation is won first and foremost on our knees.

Through prayer, we can reclaim a generation from the enemy's efforts to sow confusion, fear, deception, perversion, unbelief, and more. Through prayer, we can invite God's Holy Spirit onto our school campuses. Through prayer, we can exercise our authority in Christ, and declare and release God's power over the lives of our students, launching them into their God-given destinies!

The purpose of this book is to serve as a call to arms and a training manual to mobilize a mighty prayer force in the war over our schools and children. It is designed to impart hope and inspire your prayers as you hold up this emerging generation before Almighty God. Not only is this guide the result of substantial research, but we also have interviewed teachers, principals, administrators, and heads of educational organizations to obtain first-hand reports of what is actually happening, in real-time, in our classrooms, schools, and academic governing bodies.

Today's students need our prayers for strength, wisdom, protection, purity, and the preservation of their innocence. Schoolteachers and administrators need wisdom and courage to push back against immoral guidelines and curricula that promote ungodly ideologies and behaviors. Legislators, too, need wisdom and courage to prevail when legislation comes through asking for a vote to promote these programs. We will be covering these topics and more in the days ahead as you pray through this book either individually or with a group.

It's time for us to pick up our spiritual weapons of warfare and contend for the preservation of our children's and grandchildren's hearts, minds, and destinies. It is time to reclaim a generation!

Thank you for standing in the gap for the next generation,

Cheryl Sacks

Step onto the Battleground for Our Schools

7/31/23 ✓

Day 1: CALLING WATCHMEN AND GATEKEEPERS

"The education of youth should be watched
with the most scrupulous attention . . .
[It] lays the foundations on which both
law and gospel rest for success."
NOAH WEBSTER

"I looked for someone to stand up for me
against all this, to repair the defenses
of the city, to take a stand for me and stand
in the gap to protect this land
so I wouldn't have to destroy it. I
couldn't find anyone. Not one."
(EZEKIEL 22:30, MSG)

Noah Webster, the historic American patriot and originator of the classic *Merriam-Webster Dictionary*, has been called "the Father of American Scholarship and Education." I wonder what Noah Webster would think if he were to show up in American schools today?

I believe he would be shocked and saddened beyond belief.

We do well to remember that *"we do not wrestle against flesh and blood, but against principalities, against powers, against the rulers of the darkness of this age, against spiritual hosts of wickedness in the heavenly places"* (Eph. 6:12, ASV). What then should Christians do to hold back the onslaught of tyranny surreptitiously directed against our children? Hiding our heads in the sand certainly has not worked.

11

In the Old Testament, we read about the roles of watchmen—who stood on the walls of cities to sound the alarm about impending enemy attacks—and gatekeepers, who stood at the outer entrance of homes and either admitted or turned away any strangers or visitors who might approach the dwelling while the family was sleeping. God told Isaiah, *"Go, set a watchman; let him announce what he sees. When he sees riders, horsemen in pairs, riders on donkeys, riders on camels, let him listen diligently, very diligently"* (Isa. 21:6–7, ESV).

This is a role that we all can take on, as watchmen and gatekeepers over our schools and homes, to "listen diligently, very diligently." We need to be alert to what is going on in our classrooms and school districts so we can be well-informed and pray specific targeted prayers:

- We need to know what curriculum is being taught in our local schools and who is on the textbook committees making the decisions.
- We need to know what books are on the library shelves.
- We need to know which speakers are coming in to address our children.
- We need to know what is on the agenda at our local school board meetings—and to attend those meetings.
- We need to know what legislation is being proposed and passed in our governments relating to schools.

We also can fulfill the roles of watchmen and gatekeepers both in the natural and the spiritual realms:

- We can close spiritual doors to the enemy through our prayers.
- We can pray prayers of protection around our children's lives and schools.
- We can pray for revelation and exposure of the enemy's hidden schemes and deceptions (see Luke 12:2–3) and subversive efforts to separate children from the influence of their parents. (See Day 5: Guarding Our Children's Innocence.)

Noah Webster's centuries-old exhortation—"The education of youth should be watched with the most scrupulous attention"—should speak to us today. It is absolutely the responsibility of the older generation to guard over the spiritual and moral condition of the younger.

Are you willing to be a watchman? Are you willing to be on the alert, informed, and actively engaged in sounding the alarm and resisting the enemy's attacks? Are you willing to be one who "stands in the gap"?

Let's start by asking forgiveness—as parents, grandparents, teachers, coaches, church and community leaders—for abandoning our posts on the wall and failing to be the gatekeepers over our children and our school systems.

Let's Pray

- Lord, we confess that we, the generation who has gone before, failed to maintain our post on the wall, leaving the younger generation vulnerable. There were no strongmen at the gates, and the enemy walked right in. God, forgive us.

- We ask You to raise up spiritual watchmen (fathers, mothers, teachers, school leaders) who will watch, pray, and be a voice for truth in our schools.

- We commit to fervently pray, actively engage, and become informed about what is going on in our schools and school districts. We commit to sound the alarm when we see things going on in our schools which are harmful to our children.

- In Jesus' name, we pray that "nothing is covered up that will not be revealed, or hidden that will not be known" (Luke 12:2, ESV). Bring to light every evil plan that would bring destruction to our students and give us the wisdom in how to pray and the courage to speak up and stand against it.

Day 2: RESTORING EXCELLENCE IN EDUCATION

"Choose my instruction instead of silver,
knowledge rather than choice gold,
for wisdom is more precious than rubies, and
nothing you desire can compare with her . . .
I love those who love me, and those who seek me find me.
With me are riches and honor, enduring
wealth and prosperity . . ."
(Proverbs 8:10–12, 17–18, niv)

The students of today are the leaders of tomorrow. Of course, it's our desire that the future leaders being educated in our nation's schools and released into our communities to serve and lead will be well-equipped for the task. Alarmingly, when one looks deeply into the matter, we find many reports telling us the opposite.

While we rejoice that 80 percent of high school seniors obtain a diploma, on closer examination it becomes evident that they are not mastering the subject matter and are unprepared for their next step in life.

It seems that students are being socially promoted when they should be held back and repeat work they have not mastered. As they are moved ahead without demonstrating mastery, these students are at a distinct disadvantage. They cannot complete grade-level work and keep up with their classmates. They have a heightened chance of falling behind and dropping out of high school or college.

While this academic decline has been going on for some time behind the scenes, the COVID-19 pandemic, which had children distance-learning from their kitchen tables, brought to the spotlight shocking revelations. Parents discovered that instead of being taught the basics—reading, writing, and arithmetic—their kids were being fed lessons on highly divisive topics of questionable academic benefit. All the while, less than one-half of graduating seniors can proficiently read or even complete math problems.[1]

Many critics of the system believe that the major problem with public education in America today is a lack of focus on results. Students are simply no longer expected to meet high standards.

In the midst of the COVID-19 crisis, there was an effort to move students away from an excellence in academics to "soft skills" of social interaction and emotion. To achieve this goal, educators built on a soft skills program, the Every Student Succeeds Act (ESSA). Ulrich Boser, the senior fellow at the Center for American Progress (CAP), praised ESSA when he said, "This law calls for a well-rounded education and a shifting away from the narrow focus on academics. It's the human side of education." In lockstep with the CAP, the NEA (National Education Association) praised ESSA as an excellent program for the future workforce.[2] This explains a lot. The move away from academic excellence didn't just happen; it was intentional.

Additionally, across the education system at large, there has been a steering away from teaching critical thinking skills, which used to be one of the hallmarks of what was considered a "good" education— that is, that students not only acquire facts, but also develop the skills needed to analyze the information and make wise and accurate inferences, judgments, and conclusions.

Developing good critical thinking is crucial for protecting us from leaping to false conclusions (or acting based on wrong information).

1. Michael T. Nietzel, "Low Literacy Levels Among U.S. Adults Could Be Costing the Economy $2.2 Trillion A Year," *Forbes*, September 9, 2020, https://www.forbes.com/sites/michaelnietzel/2020/09/09/low-literacy -levels-among-us-adults-could-be-costing-the-economy-22-trillion-a -year/.
2. Nancy Huff, "The Dangers of Social, Emotional Learning," *Intercessors for America*, March 1, 2022, https://ifapray.org/blog/the-dangers-of-social -emotional-learning/.

Although the label "critical thinking" did not exist back then, the Founding Fathers learned critical thinking from their studies of history, science, religion, philosophy, and from their own life experiences.

Thomas Paine once warned, "Reason obeys itself; ignorance submits to what is dictated to it."

Today, our students are not being taught the critical thinking skills that served past generations of well-educated citizens so well, including knowing how to ask the right questions in context. Rather, many students, by contemporary educational methods, are being conditioned to passively accept information that is spoon-fed to them. Instead of being trained to think for themselves, they are often encouraged to learn in groups and to arrive at a consensus before submitting their answers. Much of today's teaching directs students' spirits and intellects away from the Lord and toward ungodly and destructive philosophies and worldviews, including pushing socialism and transgenderism, and even encouraging children to keep secrets from their parents.

These concerns run the entire spectrum of our education system and are growing. Let's stand in agreement for academic excellence in our public, private, and home schools, and in our universities, and for the development of students' critical thinking skills, that they may reach their full potential and fulfill their God-given destinies.

Let's Pray

- Father, we lift before You the schools across our nation, from kindergartens to universities. We pray they would adhere to high standards that will properly equip students for the next steps in their careers and in life.
- We pray Your Word in Proverbs 8:1–21 over our students. God, make our students' time in the classroom count—may You maximize their time and impart supernatural wisdom. Your Word says that with wisdom comes good judgment,

knowledge, discernment, common sense, insight, strength, and success.

- We ask You to impart a love of learning and a hunger for knowledge to our children and ignite in our students a drive for academic success. Give them a deep desire to seek godly wisdom and its blessings. We pray that our students will value their education and be so motivated that they will let nothing stand in the way of graduating! May they be lifelong learners who excel in their respective fields.

- Impress on educators the need to develop students' critical thinking skills. Help our students acquire and hone the needed skills to not only memorize facts, but to also analyze them, evaluate them, and hold them up to the light of Your truth.

- We ask You to supernaturally provide fresh, innovative solutions *from Heaven* at both the state and local levels in how to raise our graduation rates and increase competency in academics. We need future leaders who are well-equipped for the task. May we educate and equip our students in a way that empowers them to thrive.

Day 3: DEFENDING TRUTH
IN CURRICULA

"So justice is driven back, and
righteousness stands at a distance;
truth has stumbled in the streets, honesty cannot enter."
(ISAIAH 59:14, NIV)

"Then you will know the truth, and
the truth will set you free."
(JOHN 8:32, NIV)

Truth, in our culture as well as our schools, is under attack. In fact, in the face of the constant barrage of untruths and half-truths that have infiltrated and dominated our news, schools, entertainment, and academia in recent years, it has been said that we actually live in a "post-truth era." Does this mean the truth has been mysteriously lost, and that it cannot be found? Of course not. It does mean that the truth must be sought out and contended for like never before.

Many, if not most, textbooks have been drastically revised to present a new view of American and world history. In the last few years, the faith and godly principles of our Founding Fathers have been censored from our textbooks. Though our Founding Fathers were far from perfect, many were devout Christians who practiced their faith in their roles in government. Today our Christian heritage is disappearing from textbooks. The valiant fight of our forefathers, who gave up everything to secure our religious freedom, is no longer celebrated. Students are being groomed to hate rather than love our nation.

We have seen statues across our country pulled down, history revised and erased, and a new mentality of "oppressor versus the oppressed" forced on our schools through controversial and divisive teaching. Science classes teach that humans are the result of millennia of evolutionary processes, absent the hand and guidance of God.

Additionally, through sex education classes, children as young as elementary-aged are being taught about marriage, identity, and sexuality "norms" that are outside of God's biblical plan for us. With our country leaning more and more toward moral relativism, students are being taught in their schools that morality is up to them to decide. As a result, research shows that now, more than ever, moral convictions are waning in today's society.

School curricula are quickly moving away from being purely and objectively educational. In fact, it is difficult to find a curriculum, in almost any subject, that is purely instructional. This has become a huge business. In particular, many people and companies are getting rich in the lucrative selling and distributing of SEL (Social Emotional Learning) curricula to school districts.

Of special note: while the term SEL sounds good on the surface, it expands the role of the school and teacher to surreptitiously influence a student's beliefs, attitudes, and values, most often in a direction away from biblical foundations. The danger of SEL lies with the form and substance of the programs, as the tendency is to teach students to embrace New Age techniques. Also, SEL can serve as a catch-all umbrella under which different social, emotional, and mental health programs may operate. Public school administrators have the authority to implement any program they deem fit under the SEL category—i.e., gender choice, and sexuality. Not concerned about morals, the potential dangers of SEL loom large and dark over our children.[3]

SEL curriculum is adopted by many school districts, and teachers are required to teach the recommended content, taking time away from academic subjects.

---

3. Huff, "The Dangers of Social, Emotional Learning."

Our children are our most vulnerable population when it comes to the truth. They are dependent upon us to protect their minds and hearts from that which would direct their spirits and intellects away from the Lord and toward ungodly and destructive philosophies and worldviews. Take Canada, for example: the federal government's health department is using taxpayer money to fund the creation of a children's activity book on assisted suicide.[4] Don't think it can't happen in the United States of America!

No longer can we simply trust the systems in our nation to teach the objective, defensible truth and godly values to our children. We must be on the alert, practically and spiritually.

May our Christian teachers be discerning, stand firm in their convictions, and be a light in the darkness, pointing our students to God's truth!

Let's Pray

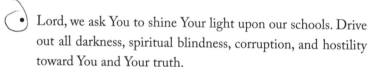

- Lord, we ask You to shine Your light upon our schools. Drive out all darkness, spiritual blindness, corruption, and hostility toward You and Your truth.
- We pray all attempts to use curricula in our schools as a way to disciple our young people in humanism, moral relativism, and other godless ideologies would be stopped.
- Heavenly Father, we pray for teachers and parents. Give them discernment to recognize deception and false ideologies, and the faith and courage to fight for truth and push back against the sources of confusion.

---

4. https://nationalpost.com/news/canada/canada-funded-this-assisted -suicide-activity-book-for-children. Accessed January 30, 2023.

- We ask for teachers and school boards to select curricula that preserve our godly heritage as a nation. We pray for the selection of textbooks that present godly values. We specifically pray for textbook committees in Texas and California, as they influence the selection of textbooks throughout the nation.

- Father, when teachers and students are confronted with subject matter that goes against their biblical values, we call upon You to give them courage. We pray for administrators and school board members, that they would be gatekeepers of truth in their school districts, and that the lies of the enemy would not get past them.

- We declare that the efforts of those who are trying to create curricula and initiatives in our schools to actively promote lies and anti-God philosophies and activities will be thwarted and defeated at every turn.

- We ask that You increase discernment, Lord, in even the youngest of students, and that they would learn to correctly handle and apply the Word of Truth to everything they learn, no matter what the subject matter is (see 2 Tim. 2:15).

- We proclaim, in the powerful name of Jesus, that this generation will rise up as warriors for truth, take back the ground the enemy has stolen, and reclaim their godly heritage in our nation!

Day 4: OVERCOMING ADVERSITY, CASTING VISION

"Vision is the #1 predictor of success in school.
It's much more predictive than test scores."
JOHN HUPPENTHAL, FORMER ARIZONA
SUPERINTENDENT OF PUBLIC INSTRUCTION

"Where there is no vision, the people perish . . ."
(PROVERBS 29:18, KJV)

O ur sense of vision is a highly motivating factor in persevering through the highest levels of adversity. If we don't have a vision, as the writer of Proverbs points out, we "perish." We lose hope. We give up.

Apart from a vision from God, there is much to be overwhelmed by in our schools and world right now. A God-given vision will help us summon the motivation we need to persevere.

Our students and schools are facing deep levels of adversity. Many schools are overwhelmed with helping students who may require additional help due to their home circumstances, such as lack of parental presence or support, or poverty. They may be immigrants or refugees from different parts of the world. Many of these students have never attended school and are struggling to grasp a new language in addition to their own. Teachers face an enormous challenge in trying to include and educate children from such a variation in educational backgrounds and families of origin.

When I was a high school teacher, in a school riddled with gangs, drugs, violence, and suicide, I asked God to give me His vision for my school. I asked Him to give me creative ideas for the class of low performers I was teaching at the time.

In response to my prayer, the Lord put into my hands a school-approved curriculum. Though not overtly Christian, it was founded on biblical principles that motivated my students toward success, and changed their lives. We can pray that God will do the same for other Christian teachers in our school systems. We can pray that our students will overcome every adversity that would hold them back. We can pray that God will give principals solutions from Heaven for the many problems their schools face.

Across the nation, there are schools struggling with any number of issues. We know that obstacles such as poverty, lack of access to transportation, addiction and substance abuse within the home, broken families, depression and other mental illnesses, generational curses, familial expectations and norms, undiagnosed learning disabilities, racial inequality, homelessness, and more, can all be mitigating factors in the academic success of any student. However, God, through His supernatural power, can make a way—if we will ask for, and implement, His vision.

Let's Pray

Father, Your Word tells us that without a vision people perish (see Prov. 29:18).

- Lord, we pray for VISION for administrators, principals, teachers, parents, and students! Give them Your vision of what their schools can become and stir their faith and hope to action. Let them see that NOTHING is impossible with God, no matter how bad the situation!
- Father of Light, we ask You to plant a vision within our students to see academic success as a real possibility in their lives. Give them a vision to overcome the challenges they live with.
- We pray for mentors and tutors to come alongside each one who is struggling and give them the educational support and vital encouragement needed to finish their schooling.

- Please open the windows of Heaven over our struggling schools, for finances and good staff, that they would receive a blessing they can't contain! Lord, we ask that You would be glorified when their needs are supernaturally met.
- Help our students who are struggling—whether with learning disabilities or with troubled families or anything else that would hinder them. We pray that You would restore their confidence and motivation, and that failures and setbacks would not discourage them. And we ask that You release the specialized teachers these students need.
- Encourage all who feel like giving up to press through to victory, we pray, in Jesus' name.

Day 5: GUARDING OUR CHILDREN'S INNOCENCE

"So God created man in his own image,
in the image of God he created him;
male and female he created them."
(Genesis 1:27, esv)

Sexuality, once an educational responsibility of parents, has moved not just into the *main*stream of education, but to the *ex*treme. Not only are today's students being exposed to extremely graphic sexually themed material in some districts in the name of "sex ed," but they are also being exposed to pressure to accept and embrace transgenderism.

Some schools and public libraries have been bringing in drag queens to teach students about alternative lifestyles, calling them "models of diversity." One program has come to be known as "Drag Queen Story Hour."[5] At first, these individuals were teaching, enter-

5. "Drag Queen Ed," *Parents' Rights in Education*, https://www .parentsrightsined.org/drag-queen-ed.html. Accessed February 27, 2022,

taining, and educating kids simply about being transgender. This was certainly bad enough. But now their activities have quickly accelerated. Drag Queen Story hour, in some instances, now includes lewd singing and provocative dancing. Most parents do no not know the extent of the grooming taking place in their children through this activity. Drag performers continue to push the bounds of sexual innuendo as they deceitfully deem such performances "kid friendly."[6]

There are LGBTQ+ curricula being written and taught in public schools across the nation. According to Blaze Media, a North Carolina preschool teacher used LGBTQ-themed flash cards to instruct her students to read. One flash card apparently showed a pregnant man. In Delaware, one school district's curriculum includes the book *Jacob's New Dress* for K–3 students. The text is included as part of the district's Social Emotional Learning (SEL) curriculum (mentioned in Day 3), which teaches progressive social ideology on race and gender to primary students.[7]

An incident at a middle school in California involved two teachers who stalked students online to identify those they felt would "benefit" from attending the school's LGBTQ club. They recruited a 12-year-old student without telling the student's parents. The punishment for the two teachers equated to a minor hand slap. The teachers who used the internet to find vulnerable children to mentor into becoming transgender did not lose their jobs or suffer suspension even after parents brought the issue to the school board's attention.[8]

Angry parents in similar situations have learned that punishment evades public school perpetrators because powerful institutions

6. https://www.azpolicy.org/2023/01/13/a-drag-on-society/.

7. Cullen McCue, "K–3 SEL Curriculum in Delaware County Includes 'Jacob's New Dress,'" *National File*, April 4, 2022, https://nationalfile.com/k-3-sel-curriculum-in-delaware-county-includes-jacobs-new-dress/.

8. https://thehill.com/changing-america/respect/diversity-inclusion/587660-teacher-who-stalked-students-online-for-lgbtq/. Accessed January 30, 2023.

support them in their immorality—the U.S. Department of Education and the National Education Association are two chief supporters of this ideology. These organizations provide tools for teachers, counselors, and administrators to assist students with gender transition. In reality, many times they are the ones seeding the confusion through counseling sessions that encourage children to question their gender—all without the parents' knowledge or consent.

Moreover, there is a growing movement afoot to provide "Transition Closets" in schools, most often without the knowledge of parents. Children, according to one teacher who supports the program, "come to school wearing the clothes their parents approve of, and then swap out into the clothes that fit who they 'truly are.'"[9] These programs provide videos teaching girls how to bind their breasts so that they appear more masculine; one recently received a grant from the Arkansas LGBTQ+ Advancement Fund. The grant will be used "to provide gender-affirming clothing and accessories for transgender and non-binary Arkansans."[10]

Sex education has radically transformed in the last handful of years, morphing from talking about contraception and how to prevent sexually transmitted diseases (STDs) to teaching kids how to engage in all kinds of sexual behavior. Today's explicit sex education has gone way past the "facts of life."

It is no surprise that student sexual activity, pregnancies, pornography use, STDs, gender dysphoria (confusion about sexual identity), and homosexuality continue to explode in our young people. It

---

9. https://www.dailywire.com/news/california-school-creates-transition
-closet-allows-students-to-swap-out-of-clothes-parents-approve-of.
Accessed January 30, 2023.
10. "School Thinks Secret 'Transition Closets' Will Help Kids with
Transgender Identity," *Partially Politics*, February 22, 2022, https://
partiallypolitics.com/2022/02/school-thinks-secret-transition-closets-will
-help-kids-with-transgender-identity/.

is probably fair to say this is the most sexually confused and conflicted generation our society has ever seen.

Let's Pray

- Lord, we recognize there is a spiritual agenda to destroy the innocence and purity of our children, to corrupt them, and to lead them down the wrong path with regard to their God-given sexuality and identity.
- God, as we face these enemy forces that would lead our students into sexual sin, we declare that You have promised to preserve the godly inheritance of parents and our nation—and that heritage is our children.
- We take authority in Jesus' name over every wicked spirit that brings these messages of corruption, perversion, and immorality to our precious children. This day, we ask for Your deliverance for our schools and our children from these enemy forces.
- We pray these graphic sexual curricula would not be approved for use in our schools, that "clubs" that promote perverted ideologies would be canceled and prohibited, and that teachers with activist agendas to corrupt our youth would be exposed and dismissed, in Jesus' name.
- We pray that laws for curriculum transparency would be enacted in every state. We pray that teachers, school boards, administrators, and counselors would be required (and held accountable) to notify parents regarding surveys offered to students, books assigned to be read, or speakers invited. We pray that all deception and efforts made in secrecy to influence and corrupt our children would be exposed and brought into the light, in Jesus' name (see Matt. 10:26; Luke 12:2).
- Lord, we pray that Your Spirit would fill our children with a desire for purity. Help them to stand strong against peer pressure and the lies of the enemy in our culture. Give them

strength to resist temptation, and to look for and seize the way of escape You always provide.

Day 6: PROTECTING OUR SCHOOLS FROM VIOLENCE

"Because you have made the LORD *your dwelling place—the Most High, who is my refuge—no evil shall be allowed to befall you . . ."*
(PSALM 91:9–10, ESV)

Praying for the safety and security of our schools is a unifying opportunity to engage our community in prayer. We all remember the tragic school shootings our nation has been through and desire to avoid these occurrences in our own communities. With these fears in their hearts, many parents send their kids to school each day wondering if they'll be safe in their classrooms.

We may feel helpless, wondering what else we can "do." Remember that prayer is not inaction; it is our greatest action. When we pray, we are not simply asking God to protect our children and schools from violent attacks—we are actually battling the evil forces behind these kinds of attacks. Prayer is our greatest weapon against evil.

We cannot wait until tragedy strikes to decide to pray. This is not the time for passivity!

We can cover our local schools all year long, from the very beginning of the year to the end, with prayers of protection for our students, our teachers, and our emergency responders.

Let's declare Psalm 91 over our campuses and over the entire school year:

"Whoever dwells in the shelter of the Most High will rest in the shadow of the Almighty. I will say of the LORD*, 'HE IS MY REFUGE AND MY FORTRESS, my God, in whom I trust.'*

"Surely he will save you from the fowler's snare and from the deadly pestilence. He will cover you with his feathers, and under his wings you will find refuge; his faithfulness will be your shield and rampart.

"You will not fear the terror of night, nor the arrow that flies by day, nor the pestilence that stalks in the darkness, nor the plague that destroys at midday.

"A thousand may fall at your side, ten thousand at your right hand, but it will not come near you. You will only observe with your eyes and see the punishment of the wicked.

"If you say, 'The LORD is my refuge,' and you make the Most High your dwelling, no harm will overtake you, no disaster will come near your tent.

"For he will command his angels concerning you to guard you in all your ways; they will lift you up in their hands, so that you will not strike your foot against a stone. You will tread on the lion and the cobra; you will trample the great lion and the serpent.

"'Because he loves me,' says the LORD, 'I will rescue him; I will protect him, for he acknowledges my name. He will call on me, and I will answer him; I will be with him in trouble, I will deliver him and honor him. With long life I will satisfy him and show him my salvation.'" (Psalm 91, NIV)

Let's Pray

- Dear Heavenly Father, we pray for the security of our students, asking You to protect them from harm and evil.
- Grant strategy and wisdom to our teachers, principals, and school administrators, that they may be able to set the right security protocols, to prevent tragedy from occurring. Alert them to every potential threat, to prevent every act of violence, apprehending those who are planning such evil.

- We lift up our local law enforcement and first responders, that they too may be alert against potential threats, and that You will position them at the right place and time to stop any potential threats. In Jesus' name, we pray for *angelic security forces* over our campuses, and we declare that the Holy Spirit will be a *wall of fire* around our schools, and the glory in their midst (see Zech. 2:5)!

- We declare that *every scheme of the enemy* hidden in darkness will be brought out into the light. Expose every plan of violence, terror, and wickedness, and prevent them from being carried out on our school campuses (see Matt. 10:26).

- Lord, we ask that Your presence would rest on our schools and create an atmosphere of safety, protection, and life. We know that in the presence of the Good Shepherd, there is perfect peace. We ask You to quiet our children's hearts and give them rest, just as sheep in green pastures (see Psalm 23).

- We ask that You radically encounter those who plot evil, who have allowed the seeds of anger, violence, hatred, and death to take root in their hearts. We pray that your Holy Spirit would dispel the darkness in their hearts—that the power of Your love would soften their hearts and draw them to repentance!

- Lord, we speak Your peace and protection over all of our school campuses (kindergarten to universities) this entire school year.

Day 7: SPEAKING UP AND STEPPING IN

"Speak up for those who cannot speak for themselves . . ."
(PROVERBS 31:8, NIV)

"If anyone causes one of these little ones—
those who believe in me—to stumble,
it would be better for them to have a large
millstone hung around their neck
and to be drowned in the depths of the sea."
(MATTHEW 18:6, NIV)

Across the nation, a wave of fervent prayer for our schools is rising like never before. But what's unprecedented is the extent to which intercessors are also "putting feet" to their prayers.

Record numbers of parents are showing up to speak out at city councils and school board meetings, joining education action groups or running for office. And for the first time ever, the crisis in our classrooms is superseding political affiliations and uniting fathers, mothers, and grandparents.

Across the nation, concerned parents and grandparents are running for every position from mayor to governor in order to protect children and the rights of parents to know what is happening in their children's classrooms. Politicians, school board members, and school officials who are not listening to their concerns are being removed from their positions and voted out of office.

In Virginia, school administrators refused to talk to parents upset by pornographic and sexually explicit material in public school libraries! Then-governor Terry McAuliffe stated in response, "I don't think parents should be telling schools what they should teach."

This cost him the governor's mansion.

In Wisconsin, the Eau Claire Area School District was recently sued in federal court by parents objecting to school policies that promote students' gender transitioning without the notification or involvement of their parents! Shockingly, the district's official Gender Support Plan states: "Remember, parents are not entitled to know their kid's identities. That knowledge must be earned . . . we must not act as stand-ins for oppressive ideas/behaviors/attitudes, even and especially if that oppression is coming from parents."[11]

One mother in the Phoenix area spoke out and stepped up in a dramatic way. Dressed as a cat, she addressed her local school board meeting and voiced her concerns about a male school board member who was dressing in his deceased wife's clothing and identifying as a woman. The mom asked the parents and members of the school board who were attending the meeting whether they would address her as a cat if she identified as one.

"Wearing ears, whiskers, and a tail does not make me a cat; neither does wearing lipstick and a skirt make this man a woman," she pointed out. Her efforts paid off. She later received a surprising amount of community support after confronting the school board. Ultimately, the male school board member was removed from his post. Victory![12]

Please hear me. I am *not* suggesting that you attend the next school board meeting dressed as a cat. I *am* saying that if we don't speak up and step in to push back against ungodly, destructive values

---

11. Sam Shilts, "Parent Group Files Lawsuit Against Eau Claire School District Over Gender Identity Policy, *News8000.com*, September 7, 2022, updated January 24, 2023.

12. "Mom Dresses Up As a Cat at a School Board Meeting to Prove a Point," https:youtube.com; December 15, 2022. Stephen M Lepore, 'I'm a cat. Meow, meow: Mom dresses as a CAT and says she identifies as one in protest over trans school board member who 'wears his deceased wife's clothing in front of school kids,' Dailymail.com, updated December 16, 2022.

in our schools, those with evil intent—who are pushing harmful agendas upon our children—*will* speak up, step in, and prevail.

Do you think these destructive efforts against our children can't happen in your school district? Chances are, they already have.

Often, as we intercede, God will call us to be the answer to our own prayers. Prayer might open up the way, but someone must come in and "occupy" the territory (physical or spiritual) for which we are praying. We must do more than fight a few battles; we must be present inside of, and bring godly values into, the places we want to see transformed.

This is what God told Joshua when he was getting ready to lead the people to go in and take possession of the land God had promised them. God told Joshua, *"Every place where you set your foot will be yours"* (Deut. 11:24, NIV), and *"I will give you every place where you set your foot, as I promised Moses"* (Josh. 1:3, NIV).

We praise God for the victories already won as believers have stepped into the fray and taken back territory for the Kingdom. For example, just recently, in a significant "religious freedom" decision from the U.S. Supreme Court, the high court ruled six to three that a public high school in Washington State violated Coach Joe Kennedy's rights when he was disciplined and ultimately fired for taking a knee and praying quietly at the 50-yard line after football games. A lawsuit followed, and seven years later, our nation's highest court agreed with our U.S. Constitution that Kennedy's religious rights had been violated.[13]

This decision importantly corrects the mistaken impression of many that religious speech and actions must be suppressed to avoid the First Amendment's prohibition of "establishment of religion." The

13. Ron Blitzer, "Coach Joe Kennedy Celebrates Supreme Court Win," *Fox News*, June 27, 2022, https://www.foxnews.com/politics/coach-joe-kennedy -celebrates-victory-supreme-court.

majority opinion, written by Justice Neil Gorsuch, says, "That reasoning was misguided."

This ruling should give hope and encouragement to Christian employees of our public schools, clarifying a First Amendment issue that has troubled our education system for decades. It will, for example, protect teachers who bow their heads to give thanks over their lunch in the cafeteria or wear a cross around their neck. The Supreme Court's majority opinion mentioned those examples specifically.

This ruling would also apply to students who wish to pray at sporting events or on school campuses, on their own time, or who desire to place a Christian sticker on their backpack or binder. It applies to any school personnel who speak out on a matter of public concern while on school grounds but in a non-teaching situation, such as when teachers or school support staff respond to a personal question from a student or another teacher about a matter of faith. "The Constitution neither mandates nor tolerates that kind of discrimination," Gorsuch wrote.

We can rejoice in this tremendous victory in upholding religious liberty in our public schools. This results not only from excellent legal representation and the application of godly justice by the Supreme Court, but because of the concerted, fervent intercession of the body of Christ as this lawsuit made its way through the courts for over seven years!

Let's continue to intercede together and reclaim this young generation. Our prayers are making an incredible difference. Praise God!

We must not only pray for our schools; we need to speak out and step in! We need to become an active part of reforming our schools and school systems. The organization Moms for Liberty, for example, was founded by two moms who are mobilizing an army of mothers fighting for their kids and parental rights. This grassroots organization has exploded to more than 100,000 members, with nearly 250 chapters in 42 states and more added weekly as parents rise up to speak out about ungodly agendas in schools.

There was a season when our ministry team at BridgeBuilders International rented school auditoriums and prayed and worshiped in 26-hour prayer vigils inside Arizona high schools. We labored all night in intercession every weekend that fall. With broken hearts, we cried out to God for a variety of needs: food for the students, more teachers, money for repairs of the buildings, new sports equipment, and better test scores. In the midnight hours, we worshiped and contended together against suicide, depression, and despair.

At one high school, about one to three students a month were overdosing on OxyContin. The school, ranked in the bottom 25 percent academically in the state, was on probation from the Arizona Department of Education.

Immediately following our 26 hours of on-site prayer, the police came to the school and conducted a routine drug search. For the first time in anyone's memory, they found nothing! Three months later after another search, still no drugs. Even six years afterward, there were no more overdoses.

We saw dramatic results! This high school no longer ranks toward the bottom of the scale academically. Within one year, it moved to the *top* 25 percent, and also received an *A-plus* ranking from the Arizona Department of Education in the following two years.

We didn't stop there.

A nearby church stepped up to participate, and we trained 80 volunteers from its congregation to "serve, watch, and pray" on the high school campus. This included:

- Volunteering in the classroom
- Mentoring students
- Serving as hall and cafeteria monitors
- Supervising after-school activities and sporting events

While on campus or at after-school activities, these volunteers kept their eyes open and watched for students who appeared to be left out or who showed other signs of being in trouble. While volunteering and without drawing attention to themselves, they intentionally prayerwalked, asking God to drive out the darkness and fill the classrooms, hallways, and entire campus with His life-giving presence.

We can't put our heads in the sand! We need to be informed about what is going on in our schools and school districts. What are the needs in our schools? What are the school policies? What content is being promoted in their classrooms, textbooks, and libraries?

We need to be informed and become part of the change we want to see. Then we need to speak up, step in, and do something about it. Become familiar with your local school board candidates and where they stand on issues, since these are nonpartisan positions and their party affiliations will not appear on your ballot.

The Church is not supposed to be a "holy huddle"—rather, we are called to be agents of societal transformation. One primary way we do this is by using the spiritual authority we've been given in prayer, declaration, and godly action. Where followers of Jesus are absent, a vacuum is created. If the Church doesn't get involved on both a spiritual *and* practical level, this vacuum will surely be filled by the philosophies and values of the world.

Let's Pray

- God, please show us the needs in our schools, and show us the ways You are calling us to be the hands and feet of Jesus in them. Break the spirit of ignorance and apathy over our communities that causes us to be unaware of what is really going on in our children's classrooms.

- We fervently cry out to You to activate Your Church. Awaken Your people to get involved in the concerns and governance of our schools by voting, attending board meetings, and serving as board members! Make us "salt and light" to our local communities, and help us take responsibility for our schools, in Jesus' name.

- We call upon You, Father God, to awaken parents, grandparents, and citizens to take time to learn about the school board candidates running for office in their communities, to vote for candidates with biblical values, to show up and participate in meetings, and to respectfully hold school boards accountable.

- Lord, please remind me to pray for my children's teachers, principal, and school board members every day. Even when I do not agree with them, help me to bless and not curse them. When I need to speak up, give me grace and wisdom to act in a spirit of love that attracts Your presence and represents You well.

- Help me to find opportunities to volunteer on campus. And as I serve, anoint me to be a carrier of Your glory, Your goodness, every place I set the sole of my foot.

Those Who Mold Our Students

Day 8: FRIENDS

*"Run as fast as you can from all the
ambitions and lusts of youth;
and chase after all that is pure. Whatever builds
up your faith and deepens your love
must become your holy pursuit. And
live in peace with all those
who worship our Lord Jesus with pure hearts."*
(2 TIMOTHY 2:22, TPT)

*"Love overlooks the mistakes of others,
but dwelling on the failures of others devastates friendships."*
(PROVERBS 17:9, TPT)

"Do not be misled: 'Bad company corrupts good character.'"
(1 CORINTHIANS 15:33, NIV)

The kinds of friends a person chooses in school can set the course for the rest of their life. It is said that a person actually becomes like the three to five people they spend the most time with. Choosing friend groups is a huge part of what will make or break student success and relationships. Just one ungodly friendship can change the entire course of a young person's life, setting him on a course of pain and destruction. And just one godly friendship can introduce a young person to Jesus Christ and set him on a path of life and blessing. From romantic relationships to hierarchical "pecking orders" to racial dynamics and beyond, there is great opportunity for growth—and great opportunity for abuse. Students will encounter a variety of personalities and should be prepared to deal with them.

Student leaders in academics, sports, music, and theater—or anyone considered "cool"—have great influence on the other students. Our prayer is that dynamic student leaders will use their influence for good. Even those who are popular often feel they walk a tightrope trying to maintain their status and may be prone to compromise.

Bullying can be a huge problem on some campuses. Bullies are usually insecure and intimidate other students in order to feel powerful. Hurting people hurt people. We have all heard on the news about the epidemic of bullying and cyberbullying in schools that has even resulted in some students taking their own lives. This is an important issue that needs our prayers.

Some quiet, reserved, or less-confident students may appear to melt into the woodwork. They struggle to make friends. These students may be falling behind academically and may not feel beautiful, accepted, or worthwhile. Perhaps they are hurting from a broken family life and may have even been abused. We need to pray these students will not fall through the cracks or lapse into isolation or depression. We can pray that Christian students will reach out to them, introduce them to Christ, and establish meaningful friendships with them.

Students may also encounter the problem of gangs that are trying to establish territories in the schools. Some students may be attracted to these destructive kinds of friendship in their quest to belong. Pray that violent gangs will be unable to recruit, gain power, or carry out their operations within the boundaries of the school.

Because teachers and support staff cannot be everywhere and monitor everyone, students are often on their own to navigate these areas of socializing in schools. We can:

- ask God to protect students from damaging relationships.
- intercede for their minds to be open to God's truths about friendship, love, marriage, and the value of every human life.

- pray they learn to seek understanding and unity with others who may be different from them for whatever reason.

To the extent that teachers and curricula are involved in shaping young people's minds, we can pray that there would be alignment with God's heart and will. As young adults are experimenting with new ideas, values, and behaviors, pray that they be turned away from relationships and interactions that are damaging and hurtful to themselves and others.

Let's Pray

- Lord, we lift up our students to You (from kindergarten to universities), asking for Your help, guidance, protection, discernment, and grace as they navigate the sometimes precarious minefield of personal relationships.
- Holy Spirit, lead our children to choose positive, healthy relationships with friends and in dating. Turn them away from relationships that would be destructive or draw them away from You.
- We pray for a spirit of love and compassion that would help our children respect, honor, and accept all people based on the fact that we are all Your children, no matter where we come from, what we look like, or any other factor. You love us all unconditionally. Help our children to experience and extend that love to one another.
- As our great Defender, we ask that You shield Christian students and teachers from those who would seek to intimidate or silence them.
- We boldly come against the vindictive behavior of bullying. We pray there would be a change in the culture that feeds this maliciousness. As part of that culture change, we ask that You make Your people shine!

- Let Christians be known as courageous student champions who defend victims and can bring healing and peace into a situation. Help them to be accepting of one another so no one feels left out. We pray for those who feel alone: help them find healthy relationships and to feel a part of a company of friends.
- Raise up strong and godly leadership among Christian groups and campus clubs, we pray, and help them minister effectively to those around them. As the gospel advances on campuses, may the culture shift to one of love, respect, joy, and peace among all students.

Day 9: HOME LIFE

"He will turn the hearts of the parents to their children, and the hearts of the children to their parents; or else I will come and strike the land with total destruction."
(MALACHI 4:6, NIV)

"Fathers, do not exasperate your children; instead, bring them up in the training and instruction of the Lord."
(EPHESIANS 6:4, NIV)

Families are the cornerstone of our society and the frontline support system for students. Where this support system is strong, children thrive. Where it is weak, they struggle. Unfortunately, many families are under immense pressure from poverty, homelessness, lack of secure employment, and the challenges of single parenting.

Nearly 11 million children are living in poverty in America, according to a report from January 2021. More than 4 in 10 children live in a household struggling to cover basic expenses, and between 7 to 11 million children live in households in which they are unable to eat because of the cost of food.[14]

Additionally, the lack of stable housing has long-lasting effects that can impact health, education, and employment throughout people's lives and in future generations.[15]

Across the nation, states identified 1,280,866 students experiencing homelessness during the school year 2019-2020.[16] Without stable housing, young people are more vulnerable to mental health problems, developmental delays, and poor cognitive outcomes. Further, there is a correlation between housing instability and trauma, which can negatively impact future success. Educational outcomes for children are also improved with housing stability; young people in stable housing are less likely to repeat a grade and less likely to drop out of school.

The challenges of single-parent households can also deeply affect children. In 2017, 25 percent of US households were headed by a single parent. As of 2019, there were 15.76 million children living with their single mothers in the United States. In the same year, 3.23 million children were living with their single fathers.[17]

As we look for the root of the problem, researcher George Barna takes us right back to the home. Barna says that young people today

14. Areeba Haider, "The Basic Facts about Children in Poverty," *American Progress*, January 12, 2021, https://www.americanprogress.org/article/basic-facts-children-poverty/.

15. "The Importance of Housing Affordability and Stability for Preventing and Ending Homelessness," United States Interagency Council on Homelessness, May 2019, https://www.usich.gov/resources/uploads/asset_library/Housing-Affordability-and-Stability-Brief.pdf.

16. "Student Homelessness in America," National Center for Homeless Education, https://nche.ed.gov/wp-content/uploads/2021/12/Student-Homelessness-in-America-2021.pdf. Accessed February 27, 2022.

17. Arthur Zuckerman, "61 Single Parent Statistics: 2020/2021 Overview, Demographics & Facts," *Compare Camp*, May 26, 2020, https://comparecamp.com/single-parent-statistics/.

are at a distinct disadvantage because of their home life. Fifty percent of marriages end in divorce. This, along with out-of-wedlock births, leads to fatherlessness. Fatherlessness is associated with lower graduation rates, higher juvenile delinquency rates, unwed pregnancies, and drug and alcohol abuse.

Barna says that it is "parents to whom the Bible assigns the primary responsibility for shaping the worldview of their children," which Barna reports begins developing by a child's second birthday.[18]

"Very few Christian parents are intentionally focused on developing the worldview of their children," Barna continues.[19] (Developing a worldview means applying the Bible to our lives and cultural issues and believing the basic tenets of the faith.) But keep in mind only two percent of parents of preteens have a biblical worldview themselves. The result: only one-half of one percent of young people between the ages of 18 and 23 have a biblical worldview.

This is a coordinated attack. Here in America, the premeditated destruction of the family and specifically our children has been underway for decades. In 1963, Congressman Albert S. Herlong, Jr. read the *45 Communist Goals for America* into the Congressional Record, with a goal of sounding an alarm and issuing a warning against communist ideology. These goals included the following directives as quoted from the record:

- Discredit the family as an institution. Encourage promiscuity and easy divorce.
- Emphasize the need to raise children away from the "negative" influence of parents.

---

18. George Barna, "American Worldview Inventory 2022: A Detailed Look at How the Worldview of Parents of Preteens Misses the Mark," Arizona Christian University, April 12, 2022.

19. George Barna, "American Worldview Inventory 2022: Improving Parents' Ability to Raise Spiritual Champions," Arizona Christian University, April 26, 2022.

- Break down cultural standards of morality by promoting pornography and obscenity in books, magazines, motion pictures, radio, and TV.
- Present homosexuality, degeneracy, and promiscuity as "normal, natural, and healthy."[20]

Many children are not supervised, or they are left to fend for themselves. Bitdefender, a security technology company, has reported children under the age of 10 now account for 10 percent of all visitors to porn video sites, including mega-sites like Pornhub. According to Google Analytics, pornography searches increase by 4,700 percent when children are out of school. Tragically, only 3 percent of teenage boys and 17 percent of girls have never seen online pornography.[21]

Many students struggle in school because of turmoil at home. Their parents may be on drugs or alcohol, incarcerated, in a gang, or living with an open-door or live-in partner policy. Students may come to school having stayed up all night because of a drunken brawl in their home the night before. Single parents are raising children and there is often not enough money to make ends meet. Students may feel unloved and isolated because of their home life and think they have no one to turn to. Many of these children are not being taught right from wrong. No one has set a plumb line for them!

Let's Pray

- Father, we bring before You our students' families—those struggling and in pain, whether from divorce, poverty, unemployment, drug or alcohol abuse, or domestic violence. Bring

20. Donna Calvin, "The 45 Communist Goals as Read into the Congressional Record, 1963," BeliefNet.com, Accessed January 30, 2023.
21. Kristin MacLaughlin, "The Detrimental Effects of Pornography on Small Children," *Net Nanny*, December 19, 2017, https://www.netnanny.com/blog/the-detrimental-effects-of-pornography-on-small-children/.

healing, comfort, and provision for these broken and hurting homes.

- We pray that parents will get more involved in their children's lives and schools and that they will put the interests of their children above their own.

- We pray that children who are being verbally or physically abused at home would be rescued and given godly people they can turn to.

- Lord, we lift up to You students who are homeless and staying at shelters, on the street, or in cars. Your Father's heart is for the destitute and vulnerable, and we ask that You help these students and their families in powerful ways as only You can.

- According to Your Word in Malachi 4:6, we cry out that the hearts of the fathers be turned to their children and the hearts of the children be turned to their fathers.

- We pray for those parents who simply lack the motivation, sense of responsibility, or parenting skills to raise their children well. Break off apathy or helplessness and show them where they can find help. Please bring good parenting role models into the lives of young parents or teen moms who may not have had them while growing up.

- We lift up those parents who are doing their best but may be having to work two jobs, are single or divorced and living apart from their children, or are simply unable to be present with them as much as they would like. Pour out Your grace on them and provide Your comforting presence to the children.

- Raise up effective spiritual fathers and mothers, we pray! Bring positive, godly role models into the lives of children who need them, including grandparents, aunts and uncles, coaches, Sunday school teachers, youth leaders, and others. Give all of us a heart to invest in the next generation.

Day 10: TEACHERS

"Not many of you should become teachers, my fellow believers,
because you know that we who teach
will be judged more strictly."
(JAMES 3:1, NIV)

"A servant of the Lord must not quarrel
but must be kind to everyone,
be able to teach, and be patient with difficult people."
(2 TIMOTHY 2:24, NLT)

The quality of teachers has a *huge* impact on how much students learn. Good teachers have an extraordinarily powerful impact on their students' futures. Similarly, poor teachers can inflict lasting damage on the lives of their students.

Sadly, there is a growing teacher shortage in the United States. When indicators of teacher quality (certification, relevant training, experience, etc.) are taken into account, the shortage is even more acute, with high-poverty schools suffering the most from the shortage of credentialed teachers. Lack of sufficient, qualified teachers threatens students' ability to learn and reduces teachers' effectiveness. High teacher turnover consumes valuable economic resources that could be better spent elsewhere.[22] Many teachers report they are unable even to take an afternoon off for a doctor's appointment because of the lack of substitute teachers to provide respite. Principals

---

22. Emma García and Elaine Weiss, "The teacher shortage is real, large and growing, and worse than we thought," *Economic Policy Institute*, March 26, 2019, https://www.epi.org/publication/the-teacher-shortage-is-real-large-and-growing-and-worse-than-we-thought-the-first-report-in-the-perfect-storm-in-the-teacher-labor-market-series/.

and counselors are more and more being enlisted to serve as teachers in classrooms as numbers dwindle precariously.

Many teachers are leaving their profession for a variety of reasons. In some parts of the country, many are still facing rigid regulations related to the COVID-19 pandemic, and have grown discouraged as they've seen children suffering under the restrictions and fear-and-control-based messaging. The math and science fields are feeling the shortages keenly as gifted university students opt more and more for financially lucrative careers such as engineering.

Some teachers, who know the danger and destruction that comes with the radical curricula they are being forced to teach, struggle to know how to exercise their faith and conscience. Then, there are the teachers who are actively in support of such curricula, whom we might even call "activist teachers," as noted in Day 5. These teachers need our prayers, too, that the Holy Spirit would open their minds and hearts to the truth.

Public school teachers are working in increasingly unsafe working environments. According to federal data collected by the National Center for Education Statistics (NCES), schools are plagued with chronic absenteeism among students and teachers, significant increases in behavioral issues, and a rising incidence of verbal abuse and disrespect toward teachers.[23]

Anecdotal reports abound of teachers leaving the profession because of schools' dangerous discipline problems.[24] Unfortunately, rather than communicating support for safe teaching conditions, the National Education Association (NEA) adopted a new policy

---

23. https://nces.ed.gov/whatsnew/press_releases/07_06_2022.asp.
24. Kathryn Dill, "School's Out for Summer and Many Teachers are Calling It Quits," *The Wall Street Journal,* June 20, 2022, https://www.wsj.com/articles/schools-out-for-summer-and-many-teachers-are-calling-it-quits-11655732689?page=1.

statement that calls for an end to the "criminalization and policing of students."[25]

We should be very worried. The NEA's annual representative assembly ignored school safety and discipline and instead focused on radical policies like climate change, gender ideology, mask and vaccine mandates, and foreign policy.[26]

At its 2019 national convention, rather than focusing on better education or supporting and protecting teachers, as they promised to do, the organization passed policies to spend hard-earned teacher and staff dues on political agendas. Among the actions taken at the NEA 2019 Representative Assembly are these new business items:

- Explicit defense of the "fundamental right to abortion under Roe v. Wade" as well as for "youth" to "control their own bodies"
- Implementing radical racial politics; which instead of bringing unity, seeded division in the students' minds and in classrooms
- Advocating "professional development" training for homosexual club advisers, including how to "handle possible backlash from different stakeholders" (i.e., parents)
- Developing model state legislation to mandate an "LGBTQ+"-inclusive curriculum for K–12 students, forcing schools to subject students to homosexuality and gender indoctrination

25. Madeline Will, "Nation's Largest Teachers' Union Calls for Curbs on School Policing," *Education Week*, July 5, 2022, https://www.edweek.org /leadership/nations-largest-teachers-union-calls-for-curbs-on-school -policing/2022/07.

26. Cindy Long, "2022 NEA Representative Assembly Back and Better than Ever," *National Education Association*, July 7, 2022, https://www .nea.org/professional-excellence/conferences-events/annual-meeting-and -representative-assembly/about-ra/ra-news/2022-nea-representative -assembly-back-and-better-ever.

throughout the school day in many classes (disregarding the many families who don't agree with the curriculum)[27]

Instead of giving their money to the NEA, many Christian teachers are opting instead to join the Christian Educators Association for the resources, support, and protection they are looking for as educators (www.christianeducators.org, and see the Resource section at the back of this book).

This is a tumultuous time to be a schoolteacher. Teachers need our support, encouragement, and prayers more than ever!

Let's Pray

NOTE: If you know teachers, please pray for them by name.

- Father, we are deeply grateful for our nation's schoolteachers! Thank you for their willingness to serve the next generation and for the personal sacrifice so many make as they go above and beyond the call of duty on behalf of their students.
- Lord, raise up more teachers who will see education as a field of ministry. Increase the supply of educators with godly, qualified individuals who have a passion for learning and for the next generation. Bring alongside them qualified volunteers, parents, and support staff who will make their job easier.
- We know that our future teachers need tools to equip them for what they will be facing. Provide materials for them to use that are counter to the current cultural trends and can be placed in the hands of families and kids as well as in classrooms. Provide encouragement and support for teachers as they seek to teach authentic truth and godly realities in their classes.

27. https://www.nea.org/professional-excellence/conferences-events/annual-meeting-and-representative-assembly?type=nbi. Accessed January 26, 2023.

- Help teachers streamline their workload and prioritize what is most important. We ask you to remove bureaucratic barriers that may prevent them from teaching at their best.

- We pray for any teacher who is exhausted from the day-to-day job stress and has lost vision and enthusiasm. Fulfill Your Word, that You *"fully satisfy the needs of those who are weary and fully refresh the souls of those who are faint"* (Jer. 31:25, NET). We ask that You refresh and encourage those teachers who may be so discouraged that they are on the verge of leaving.

- We pray that good teachers would receive Your strength to remain steadfast, that they would see their profession as a God-given calling, and faithfully remain at their posts.

- We bless our teachers, in the name of the Lord, and ask for health, safety, and Your abundant blessing on them and their families—and most of all, that they would know and serve You.

- Holy Spirit, You are the ultimate Teacher, and we invite You into our classrooms and online learning experiences to lead students and teachers alike "into all truth" (see John 16:13). We lift up to You those teachers whose hearts and minds are not aligned with Your truth, and who are actively engaged in turning their students away from You and from godly principles. We pray that these teachers would come to a knowledge of the truth and experience salvation in Jesus Christ.

- We pray our teachers will know they are loved, appreciated, and essential to the health and well-being of our children and youth. Let them know how much they are valued as they leave a positive impact on our world.

Day 11: COUNSELORS AND SUPPORT STAFF

"And do not forget to do good and to share with others,
for with such sacrifices God is pleased."
(HEBREWS 13:16, NIV)

"In the same way, let your light shine before others,
that they may see your good deeds and
glorify your Father in heaven."
(MATTHEW 5:16, NIV)

Our school systems rely heavily on a vast army of crucial workers who invest in the lives and education of our children. These include paraeducators, classroom assistants, librarians, counselors, tutors, specialists, school nurses, lunchroom and kitchen staff, school bus drivers, playground monitors, crossing guards, security staff, custodial staff, office workers, and more. When these positions are not well funded, appreciated, or filled with the highest quality of personnel, our children and their education suffer in many ways.

Currently, in the United States the average student-to-school-counselor ratio is a whopping 464 to 1, according to the American School Counselor Association. Nearly 1 in 5 students—about 8 million—don't have access to a school counselor at all, with nearly three million of those students also lacking access to school psychologists, social workers, or any other type of support staff.[28]

According to the National Institutes of Health, nearly one-third of all adolescents ages 13 to 18 will experience an anxiety disorder,

---

28. Ana Connery, "School Counselor Shortage: How It Affects Your Children," *Parents Together*, September 14, 2020, https://parents-together.org/school-counselor-shortage-how-it-affects-your-children/.

and these numbers have been rising steadily. There are many reasons for this, one of which is that today's children and teens are connected constantly to social media and being bombarded by all kinds of negative messaging. Another is the barrage of false messaging and propaganda many are receiving through avenues like social media, some public school curricula, and even school staff who intentionally espouse false ideologies with the intent to sway children away from God's truth and toward deception.

Principals report that their schools are dealing with unprecedented levels of mental health issues. One Ohio middle school principal reported that in the previous year alone, eight of his students had been hospitalized with mental health issues, a number he'd never before experienced. He said multiple students had confided in him that they were hearing voices in their heads telling them to hurt people, with specific details of how to do it. He surmised these influences were demonic in nature. In the face of such an onslaught of mental health issues, counselors, teachers, and support staff report they are overwhelmed. Unequipped. Understaffed.

We need to pray for God's supernatural intervention because, just like the principal previously mentioned had experienced, many of the problems being faced in our schools are supernatural in nature. We must pray that God provides divine insight and wisdom, as well as manpower, to our school counselors and support staff who are battling on the front lines. These people fill vital roles in our schools and in our students' lives. We need to pray there are enough of them, qualified and endowed with the wisdom of God, to adequately serve our children well.

Let's Pray

- Thank You, Lord, for this army of vital workers that often goes unnoticed and unappreciated in the roles they play. These people are the glue that holds together our schools. We pray they would experience Your pleasure and blessing for their sacrifices and investment in the lives of students.

- We ask You to provide the funding needed for counseling and support programs since these positions are often the first to be cut when there are budget shortfalls.

- We ask You to direct administrators to allocate finances wisely—and avoid the waste that frequently occurs—so that all available monies can be utilized effectively for these important staffing needs.

- Perhaps more than any other support staff, counselors have the greatest impact on students' lives, influencing strategic decisions involving education, career, relationships, and morality. We pray for more qualified Christian school counselors and psychologists in our schools who will have godly values and a biblical worldview.

- Please protect the support staff personnel in every way: their finances, their safety, their health, their emotional well-being, and their families. For all the vital qualities and programs they contribute, we pray You would use them to bring wisdom, guidance, creativity, safety, nutrition, health, and order.

- May they be governed by integrity and honor and kindness in all their interactions with students and one another. Help them to always treat the students with dignity, respect, and compassion. We pray that they will experience satisfaction and significance in their jobs, and we ask You to use them in a mighty and powerful way in the lives of the students they serve.

Day 12: PRINCIPALS AND ADMINISTRATORS

"The wisdom that comes from God is first
utterly pure, then peace-loving, gentle,
approachable, full of tolerant thoughts and kindly actions,
with no breath of favoritism or hint of hypocrisy.
And the wise are peace-makers who go on quietly sowing
for a harvest of righteousness—in other
people and in themselves."
(JAMES 3:17–18, PHILLIPS)

Principals and school administrators, including school district officials, wear a lot of hats. Their leadership sets the pace and priorities for schools. They answer to a vast variety of different stakeholders who have numerous interests in their schools, which means these administrators are often under a lot of pressure to please different people with differing priorities. Budgets. Politics. School policies. Staff and student disciplinary issues. Curricular choices. Sports and extra-curricular activity policies. School health and safety protocols. These people fill multifaceted and demanding roles, and they need our prayers.

Principals and vice principals are the ones who deal with most of the discipline issues with students, a role made even more challenging with the increase of behavior and mental health issues in today's students. They are the ones who must handle personnel issues with faculty and staff and policy issues with the school district.

Of late, principals and administrators are dealing with upset, even irate, parents who are fed up with the direction our education system is headed. Some of these administrators share the parents' concerns. Others actively resist them. There is a lot of tension in school administration, and our principals and administrators bear much of the burden.

Additionally, as we reach the three-year mark of the initial wave of pandemic-induced school shutdowns, principals must deal with the repercussions. We are nowhere near "back to normal." In addition to the ongoing Covid virus—along with rising, near-epidemic rates of influenza and RSV (Respiratory Syncytial Virus)—schools have faced severe staff shortages, high rates of absenteeism, and political tensions. Furthermore, students and educators continue to struggle with mental health challenges, higher rates of violence and misbehavior, and concerns about lost instructional time.

It takes a lot for a school to run as it is intended, and the principals are the people at the head of it all. They are the ones who get their names in the paper, the ones who get the comments about how the school is doing. These days, when there are so many teacher shortages around the country, principals are regularly being thrust into the classrooms as substitute teachers—while still needing to fulfill their other obligations.

Our principals and administrators carry great burdens and responsibilities—which is why we should be praying for them on a regular basis. They need all of the help and guidance they can get!

Several studies have indicated that principals can facilitate strong school climates by helping teachers and students feel safe, valued, and emotionally supported, helping them believe their individual effort will lead to achieving academic goals. To this end, we want to support them and encourage them, as well as intercede for them.

Do you know the names of the administrators at your local school? Have you met them? Perhaps you could take a moment in the coming days to contact them. When you do, you can let them know that you will be praying for them, the staff, and the school. Ask them if there is anything specific you can be praying about.

Let's Pray

- Dear Lord, thank You for all the superintendents and school principals in my school district and in those across the United States. Please help them in their all-consuming daily responsibilities; enable them to function in a spirit of peace to bring order into their school environment and challenging situations. We ask You to expand their leadership and executive abilities. We pray You will help them implement innovative solutions to bring safety, unity, and productivity to their schools.

- Where there is turmoil, we pray our principals and administrators will be peacemakers who can bring a fair and righteous outcome in a spirit of humility.

- Give them grace to listen to the questions and concerns they will receive from families, and discernment as they respond. Help parents to be reasonable and willing to hear what our administrators have to say, recognizing that the administrators are working hard to make decisions that are safe and beneficial for all students.

- Help our school administrators find a balance between being professional and being approachable. Bless them with empathy and creativity as they strive to support and encourage their students, staff, and families.

- We pray that You, God, would encourage them. Refresh and strengthen them when they're weary and give them grace when they feel like they've reached their limit.

- May the hearts of all in leadership always put the good of our students first. Please grant our administrators an abundance of wisdom and insight as they make decisions about how to lead our schools.

Day 13: GOVERNMENT LEADERS AND EDUCATION ORGANIZATIONS

"I urge that supplications, prayers, intercessions, and thanksgivings be made for all people, for kings and all who are in high positions, that we may lead a peaceful and quiet life, godly and dignified in every way."
(1 Timothy 2:1–2, esv)

Studies show that local school boards play a critical role in the success of their districts' schools. They have tremendous authority to make decisions at a local level, including:

- Strategic planning for their community's goals and policies
- Approving curricular materials
- Being accountable to the community to make sure schools are well run
- Hiring and evaluating the district superintendent
- Overseeing the budget and salaries for employees and approving purchases

The role of school board members is one of the most important and influential in our community. School boards not only have a lasting impact on local education, but they are also typically the first step for anyone seeking higher public office as a mayor, state representative, or congressman.

As a concerned parent, taxpayer, and prayerful watchman, you can attend school board meetings in your local area, get to know your board members, pray for them, and share your encouragement, ideas, or concerns. Besides prayer, we also need to hold them accountable. Sometimes policies with great ramifications are passed without anyone knowing anything about them. In the last couple of years, awareness of this issue has increased. Many examples have made it into the national news of parents pushing back against radical school board decisions that have adversely affected schools and students. In many of these cases, this has led to greater accountability and transparency.

State licensing boards also need our prayers. Teachers must receive state licensure to be employed in public and many private schools, and that licensure is becoming harder to obtain for religious Americans. Minnesota, for example, will soon ban anyone who disagrees with radical gender identity ideologies from teaching in public schools by requiring that every state-certified teacher "fosters an environment that ensures student identities such as . . . gender identity . . . are . . . affirmed."[29] The state agency that composed these changes—Minnesota's Professional Educator Licensing and Standards Board (PELSB)—would effectively ban religious Americans from teaching in Minnesota schools by requiring that all new teachers publicly reject their faith's declaration that God has created only two sexes, male and female.

As we talk about who is influencing our students and their schools, it's important to understand the power of teachers' unions in America. As we discussed in Day 10, rather than working for better wages and working conditions, todays' teachers' unions are well-funded, highly politicized organizations that are hurting—not helping—the public education system in America and keeping even the worst teachers protected. It is the teachers' unions, the National Educators Association (NEA) and the National Federation of Teachers (NFT), that largely control the school boards in America.

Also, many people do not realize the power their governor has over their state's education system. Governors play an important role in shaping education policy in states through their power to appoint

---

29. Joy Pullmann, "Minnesota Poised to Ban Christians, Muslims, and Jews from Teaching In Public Schools," *The Federalist*, January 12, 2023, https://thefederalist.com/2023/01/12/minnesota-poised-to-ban-christians -muslims-and-jews-from-teaching-in-public-schools/.

members of their state boards of education, department of education heads and other key roles. Governors also use their authority to advocate for specific education policies and funding.

In my state of Arizona, for example, former Governor Doug Ducey advocated for and signed into law one of the country's most expansive school choice laws, the Empowerment Scholarship Account (ESA) program. ESA called for tax dollars to stay with the child rather than the school, giving parents the opportunity to send their child to the school where he or she could best succeed. Less than a year later, our newly elected governor, Katie Hobbs, is working hard to *cancel* this school choice option. If she is successful, this will eliminate education options for the children of Arizona families.[30] It's important to know where your governor stands on such issues.

Praying for our state legislators, as their roles relate to education, is another impactful way we can make a difference in our local schools. The decisions they make affect both our schools and the well-being of our students.

Praise God for the Utah legislature's bold stance in the battle over gender ideology. Not only has Utah already implemented laws to protect women's sports from activists seeking to insert biological males into women's competitions, but it is also going one step further. Importantly, the legislature is working to protect parents and children from the harmful and permanent effects of youth sex changes and gender transition treatments. Legislators in Utah have recognized the damaging implications of the affirm-only/affirm-early policy approach, implementing legislation that "prohibits performing sex-characteristic surgical procedures on a minor for the purpose of effectuating a sex change." We can pray more states follow suit.

---

30. Jason Bedrick and Corey DeAngelis, "Arizona Gov. Katie Hobbs Wants to Turn Back the Clock on School Choice," *Wall Street Journal,* January 16, 2023.

We can also pray against the influence of radical Marxist agendas of national- and state-level teachers' unions, boards of education, and state and national associations and lobby groups, such as the National School Board Association and the Superintendents' Association. On a federal level, we can lift up the U.S. Department of Education to the Lord in prayer. This is another powerful governmental agency with great influence on our teachers, prospective teachers, schools, and students. Unfortunately, a fundamental problem with the Department of Education is that it removes decision-making authority from the parents and taxpayers in local communities.

We do know from publicly available spending and achievement data that, since 1970, education spending has roughly tripled in real, inflation-adjusted terms, but student achievement has remained largely flat.[31] Only 30 percent of fourth graders in America are reading at or above grade level. This statistic alone shows how dire our educational system is in this country.[32]

Let's Pray

- Heavenly Father, we lift up our school districts and boards to You and ask for Your leadership and wisdom to be present with them as they make decisions for our schools.
- For our local school boards, we pray that Your plans and purposes for each district and school would be reflected in their long-term strategic planning, and we invite Your Spirit to be present in every school board meeting across our state.

---

31. Andrew J. Coulson, "Addressing the Critics of This Purportedly No Good, Very Bad Chart," *Cato Institute*, September 29, 2014, https://www .cato.org/blog/addressing-critics-purportedly-no-good-very-bad-chart.
32. Laurel Imer, "Radical Teaching Continues to be Pushed by Department of Education," *Campfire Colorado*, June 24, 2022, https://campfirecolorado .com/opinion/radical-teaching-continues-to-be-pushed-by-department-of -education/.

- We pray that godly people in our communities would step forward to run for the school board and take a place of leadership in this critical juncture in our nation's history as we fight for truth at all levels of our society—particularly education.

- Lord, we pray for Your answers to the obstacles that often confront our school boards: the lack of unified vision, little urgency to implement needed reforms, resistance to change, frequent member turnover that makes it difficult to follow through on long-term strategies, financial shortfalls, community apathy, disunity, and a lack of stable leadership. We pray that You would bring order, peace, and clarity in these situations.

- When confronted with issues that clearly violate their conscience and the Word of God, we pray You would empower school associations and government leaders to stand up for what is right. We break off the spirit of intimidation and release Your power, love, and sound mind over them (see 2 Tim. 1:7) to stand up for truth and real justice.

- We pray for righteous governors and legislators. Encourage them to use their power and influence to stop or slow the radical agendas that are being implanted in our schools. Let Your wisdom and discernment flow freely in them, and grant them the courage and boldness to speak and act on Your behalf.

- We pray You would raise up leaders in every educational organization at local, state, and national levels. We pray that those with ulterior motives and radical agendas would be exposed, denounced, and removed.

Day 14: THE CHURCH

"Then he said to his disciples, 'The harvest
is plentiful, but the laborers are few;
therefore, pray earnestly to the Lord of the harvest
to send out laborers into His harvest.'"
(MATTHEW 9:37–38, ESV)

Many churches and Christian ministries are finding that praying for and meeting needs in their local schools is an important way to reach children and their families for Christ, as well as to strengthen ties with their communities.

One idea is for churches to adopt their neighboring schools. Church leaders can ask their congregations to select one or more schools that God lays on their hearts and set aside time to pray specifically for that school—its issues, students, teachers, administrators, and district leaders. Your church could schedule a prayerwalk or prayer drive several times a week around the perimeter of the school of your selection. Prayerwalking or prayer driving near and around a school helps engage hearts to pray with more fervency and focus for the needs of the teachers and students. Prayer is the key that opens doors to the needed connections, such as favor with principals and teachers, that will enable us to get into the schools to meet spiritual and practical needs.

You may want to begin by reaching out to the teachers you know and finding out how you can serve them. Get to know your public school officials and staff members by name. Thank them and express appreciation for the hard work they do. Send notes and cards of appreciation to teachers in your schools. Provide modest gifts as a token of appreciation, such as coffee shop or bookseller gift cards, plants, notepads, etc. Ask how you can pray for them, and really listen.

One church in Washington State sponsors a Back-to-School Fair every August where needy families can come and receive backpacks, school supplies, clothing, haircuts, and dental checkups before school starts. There is also a "Prayer Tent" where the church's intercessory prayer team is available for students and their families to receive prayer. The majority of families who come to the event are unchurched, and many are eager to receive prayer. Afterward, many of them end up joining the church and bringing their children to the children's ministry!

You may want to consider renting the school auditorium and hosting a prayer vigil. Meet with the school principal to inquire about this. Ask him or her to tell you the school's specific needs and promise to pray for these during the event. Discuss the length of time you will need access to the building and ask about any restrictions. You can always invite the principal to the prayer vigil; they may be willing to let students and faculty know about the event.

You may want to do something like we do in Arizona by mobilizing a 21-day back-to-school prayerwalk, using this *Reclaim a Generation* book as your prayer guide. Individuals, families, and church groups can prayerwalk schools in their neighborhood or around the school they or their children attend.

We always see powerful results from our back-to-school prayer initiative. One year, right after our school prayerwalk, a woman was walking by the school her church had adopted in prayer when she noticed two strange cars in the parking lot crammed with intimidating men and the car doors wide open. Sensing something was terribly wrong, she ran into the school and alerted the principal. He locked down the building just seconds before angry men stormed the front door.

It was strategic timing, surely orchestrated by the Spirit of God—all because one church prayed.

Let's Pray

- We fervently pray You would awaken Your Church and that believers would become actively engaged in praying for their local schools and our education system. Help us see this harvest field in our own backyards and find meaningful ways to pray, serve, and reach the next generation. The Church has a message of hope to impart to our communities and schools. Show us how to do that!

- Lord, we ask that believers in local churches will pray for favor in their schools and see doors unlocked to minister inside the schools in ways they never before thought possible. Give them, and their church leaders, creative ideas for how to share the love of Jesus with teachers and students.

- We pray for favor, as the Church, to be able to start after-school Bible studies and Good News Clubs where students can freely come and hear about God's plan of salvation and His great love and design for their lives.

- Father, we pray that Your Spirit will inspire church leaders to open the doors of their facilities and provide programs like before- or after-school daycares, coffee shops, homework centers, and open gyms where church members can personally interact with kids and parents from the community.

- Lord, raise up individual believers and entire churches to partner with local schools in caring for the practical and spiritual needs of every student and their families. Send godly volunteers, mentors, tutors, and coaches to come alongside students, teachers, and their families.

- We declare that Your Church will shine brightly and glorify You in our schools through unprecedented acts of love, service, and kindness, in Jesus' name!

Ignite Spiritual Awakening on Campuses

Day 15: SHIFTING THE SPIRITUAL ATMOSPHERE

"For I will pour water on the thirsty land,
and streams on the dry ground;
I will pour out my Spirit on your offspring,
and my blessing on your descendants.
They will spring up like grass in a meadow,
like poplar trees by flowing streams."
(ISAIAH 44:3-4, NIV)

We've heard incredible testimonies about how this *Reclaim a Generation* national school prayer initiative is mobilizing people to step out in faith and prayer to change the spiritual climate in their schools. Parents, grandparents, and entire church prayer groups are turning up to pray at or near school campuses and forming intercessory prayer groups that pray together regularly for students, staff, and their schools. Teachers report that the atmospheres of their classrooms and schools are different when intercessors pray. Students are talking about spiritual things where they never did before.

Last year, immediately after a prayerwalk at her school, one elementary school teacher, who up until then had not been able to find any prayer partners, discovered that the school secretary was a Christian. They started prayerwalking together every morning. Their numbers grew, and they started meeting in her classroom every morning for prayer. It was not long before they felt the spiritual atmosphere in the entire school change! Incompetent teachers left. The heaviness in the atmosphere, which had made it challenging to even be in the school, lifted. Fighting and brawls among students stopped. There was a lighter, brighter feeling all over the school.

This same teacher, who is a music teacher, tells of even greater breakthroughs that occurred after the prayerwalking initiative. Though in previous years she had used a playlist with Christmas carols that included spiritual songs, this particular year the impact on her young students, first and second graders, was astounding.

The children heard and sang such classics as "Silent Night," "Joy to the World," and "O Holy Night." As they sang the songs, some of them stumbled over unfamiliar words like "Christ" and "Savior" when they sang the lyrics, "Christ the Savior is born."

One little boy asked, "Who is 'the Christ'?"

She told him, "Jesus is the Christ, the Anointed One."

Another asked, "Is that why we call it 'Christ-mas'?"

Another inquired, "How did Jesus die? Is He alive today?"

One child responded, "He died to take away our sins!" (Out of the mouth of babes!)

It was a holy moment. Some of the children broke out weeping during the song because the presence of the Lord was so strong. Several autistic students, and another student who had experienced deep trauma, asked for these songs to be played over and over. They called them "calming songs."

A few days later, several students broke out in spontaneous singing of "Angels Watching Over Me" (a song their teacher had taught them during a unit on folk spirituals). One child said, "If I feel angry or sad, this music helps me feel better."

In every school where this teacher has taught, she has found that it is prayer that opens the door for the Holy Spirit to come in. She finds other teachers who will pray with her, and then they invite in a "Good News Club" (Child Evangelism Fellowship) after school to work with the children. She testifies that time after time, the Lord moves through their prayers to bring favor. The principal of the school agrees to the proposal, and a teacher volunteers to sponsor and lead the club. She notes how the atmosphere in all these schools has shifted, as evidenced by tangible, measurable results.

Let us remember that the real war in our schools is over who will rule the atmosphere. Will it be the Spirit of God—or some other spirit? You might be asking how we can *know* who is ruling the spiritual atmosphere. We know that Satan comes to steal, kill, and destroy, and Jesus comes that we might have life, and have it more abundantly (see John 10:10). So, we can tell who is ruling the atmosphere based on the evidence.

Today, invite the transforming presence of God's Spirit into our schools to drive out any fear and uncertainty and replace it with a climate of peace and joy, one where our children will thrive and flourish. In an atmosphere full of God's peace and presence, our children will be able to overcome obstacles and reach their full God-given potential. In this environment, there often arises a spiritual hunger where children are asking questions and seeking answers about spiritual things. They become more open to God's Spirit working in their own hearts.

When the tangible presence of God fills a school, spirits of heaviness and hopelessness must flee!

Let's Pray

- Father, thank You for this incredible promise—that You will refresh the driest places! Where the environment has been spiritually dry and cold in our schools, we ask for streams of the Holy Spirit, the Water of Life, to pour into their hallways and classrooms.
- Where there is fear and uncertainty, we declare in Jesus' name there will be peace, confidence, and stability.
- We believe You will rain down an outpouring of Your presence that will shift the spiritual atmosphere on every school

campus across our state and nation and enable our children to thrive and flourish like strong trees growing by the riverside.

- We ask for an unprecedented, tangible presence of Your Holy Spirit in our schools, driving out the darkness and flooding the atmosphere of the classrooms with Your goodness and power!
- Lord, please give our Christian teachers creative ideas for sharing Christ within the confines of their subject matter. Make them courageous in their witness despite any opposition. Let them see undeniable demonstrations of Your power that will strengthen their own faith and inspire faith in others.
- Empower Christian students, teachers, and administrators to truly be light and salt, in Jesus' name. We ask You to touch them so powerfully that they would acknowledge publicly that they belong to You.
- Come, Holy Spirit! Soften students' hearts, instill a spiritual hunger in them, and inspire them to ask questions that will lead them to a saving faith in Jesus.

Day 16: IMPARTING GOD-GIVEN PURPOSE

"'For I know the plans I have for you,' declares the LORD, 'plans to prosper you and not to harm you, plans to give you hope and a future.'"
(JEREMIAH 29:11 NIV)

Our children and young adults are desperately looking for identity and purpose, asking questions like: *Who am I? What makes me different? What is my purpose in this world?* In fact, in America, our children and youth are experiencing an identity *crisis*.

Due to the pressure and messaging of the media—including social media such as Instagram, Facebook, Snapchat, TikTok, and the like—young people often have no idea who they are and feel compelled to try to be someone else. Oftentimes, what they see on social media tells them they're not good enough—that their clothes, their homes, their cars, and even their bodies need to be different or better. These messages are often magnified in the school environment.

Each of us is known by our Father God, who has a design for our lives within His perfect plan. However, evil forces are distorting the very core identity of our children, confusing them through the lie that they can decide whom they want to be based on "feeling" instead of living out God's original design. A lot of false information about identity, sexuality, and life purpose is being disseminated through our public schools.

I recently viewed a video interview of a young "nonbinary" teacher who was teaching a classroom of preschoolers about identity. Using a doll to reinforce the lesson, she led the children in a discussion about being a boy or a girl.

She asked the doll, "Are you a boy or a girl?"

The answer (from the doll, in the teacher's voice) was, "I'm just a *kid*."

The teacher went on to explain that some people don't know if they are a boy or a girl, and that's okay. They can be "nonbinary," in which case, we call them "they."[33]

In a similar video, a teacher explained to her class that when a child is born, even doctors don't really know the baby's gender. They make their best guess, but it is the child who will make the decision later if he or she is a boy or a girl.

Our gender is one of the core parts of our identity. God made humans "male and female" in His image (see Gen. 1:27). If kids

---

33. Jeffrey Clark, "Teacher Speaks to Children with 'Non-Binary' Doll Named 'Nash' in Video Gone Viral," *Fox News,* January 25, 2023, https://www.foxnews.com/media/teacher-speaks-children-non-binary-doll-named -nash-video-gone-viral-psychotic.

cannot be confident of this most basic component of who they are, it's no wonder they struggle with every other facet of their identity and purpose. A friend of mine related that his young niece was being taught in her elementary school that she should use others' preferred pronouns. She told him that one of her friend's preferred pronouns was "Cake."

"Cake?" he asked in surprise.

"Yes, Cake," replied his niece. "Because my friend says sometimes she feels light and fluffy!"

That may sound funny, but it's also sad. It demonstrates how confused this younger generation has become. Schools are the chief perpetrators of this by the way they are pushing preferred pronouns on children, embedding in kids' minds the idea that there is no biological gender and that such things cannot be known with certainty.

Of course, we extend God's love and mercy to people who are caught in this deception; that being said, the philosophy itself is from the very pit of hell. God's Word tells us that we have divinely powerful weapons for the tearing down of strongholds and every lofty thing raised up against the truth of God (see 2 Cor. 10:4–5). Prayer is one of those weapons we can use to tear down the strongholds of confusion, deception, insignificance, inferiority, rejection, and comparison, and replace them with affirmation of and confidence in God's unconditional love and acceptance—in the truth of His original design for a child's body and identity.

We need to not only pray, but also have frank discussions with our students and teachers about the reality of God's design, encouraging them and supporting them as they stand firm in the truth on their school campuses and in their communities. We also need to make sure they know how much God loves them, knows them personally, and has a plan for their lives.

Parents, grandparents, teachers, coaches, counselors, pastors, and youth leaders can come alongside students to reassure them that not only has God created them perfectly, but He knows them intimately (see Psalm 139:13–16). He has designed them with special gifts to equip them for the destiny and special assignments He has planned in advance for them. We can encourage them by calling out these unique gifts and reminding them they are special, loved, and destined for great things.

Let's Pray

- Lord, thank You for Your promise to bless our children. Because of Your blessing, our children will find their true identity and sense of purpose in belonging to You, their Father and Creator.
- We decree that our children will recognize, embrace, and walk in Your truth, and that they will fulfill the purpose and destiny to which You have called them. We decree that a young generation of revivalists and reformers like Joseph, Daniel, and Esther will arise!
- Please silence the negative voices telling our students they are worthless or unwanted or that they can find their identity and purpose outside of Your plan for their lives. You have a unique design and plan for every student. We ask for these plans to be preserved to give them hope and a future (see Jer. 29:11)!
- We pray that our children will have a revelation of *truth* about who they really are in You, and we ask for protection from false information about their purpose, sexuality, identity, and Your design for life.
- Give our students who are followers of Christ the courage and boldness to stand up to peer pressure and unbiblical teaching, and to push back against the culture.
- Heavenly Father, Creator of all life, You have dreamed a unique dream for every individual. Therefore, we cry out, "The destinies of our children will be preserved!" Give this

emerging generation vision and a sense of purpose regarding their future.

- Father God, it is time! Raise up sons and daughters with godly purpose and destiny to contend for the future of our nation (see Isa. 22:22). We pray they will lead the way for righteousness and justice in every sphere of cultural influence. May they, like David, fulfill the purpose of God in their generation (see Acts 13:36).

Day 17: LIFTING UP ELEMENTARY SCHOOLS

"Jesus called the children to him and said, 'Let the little children come to me, and do not hinder them, for the kingdom of God belongs to such as these.'"
(LUKE 18:16, NIV)

Elementary school is a pivotal developmental stage in the lives of our children. They are young, often anxious about their first school experience, and very impressionable.

It is during the elementary school years that students develop their personalities, learn to read and write, acquire basic math skills, and develop the beginnings of what may become lifelong friendships.

For many kids, however, elementary school can be their first exposure to bullying, teasing, cliques, and other cruel behavior. It may also be their first exposure to extreme behavior such as major tantrums and violent outbursts, which have become rampant in our elementary schools. For some kids, elementary school is their first experience away from their moms and dads, which may tempt them to "experiment" with behaviors that do not align with who they are.

These days, many children are challenged by problems that developed during the COVID-19 pandemic. In the 2021–22 school year, nearly two-thirds of teachers (64 percent) had more students who made less progress than in a typical school year. And 45 percent of teachers reported that at least half of their students ended the year a grade level behind.[34]

While this learning loss was widespread, some students were disproportionately impacted, most notably the youngest of elementary students. Moreover, because of the prolonged mask mandates, schools are now reporting increases in speech delays. During this season, children were unable to see the faces and lip movements of others, which is a necessary component of learning how to form words. The youngest students also struggled most with successfully negotiating online learning. These are formative years for developing social skills, and many of these kids were isolated. The full repercussions of these delays are only now being identified and measured.

Spiritually, the elementary school years are a strategic and vital time to minister to children. A survey cited by the International Bible Society indicates that 85 percent of Christians make their first commitment to Jesus between the ages of 4 and 14.[35] Additionally, grade school-aged children have a remarkable ability to memorize and retain information at this time of life—the perfect time and opportunity to learn about God, His ways, and His Word.

During the elementary school years, we have the opportunity to lay foundations in children's lives. We can pray for them to be reassured, protected, and affirmed, and for a plumb line of truth, justice, and confidence to be laid for them—a foundation that will last a lifetime.

---

34. "Back to School for K–12 students: Issues Ahead," U.S. Government Accountability Office, August 30, 2022, https://www.gao.gov/blog/back-school-k-12-students-issues-ahead.

35. "At What Age Do Americans Become Christian?," SNU, accessed January 27, 2023, https://home.snu.edu/~hculbert/ages.htm.

Let's Pray

- Thank You, Lord, for Your heart of love and concern, especially for our youngest children! We pray for every young student in America, as well as their teachers and aides. The Kingdom of God belongs to them, even as Your Word says.
- We ask that these tender young hearts and minds would keep their innocence and purity. We pray that You would raise up an army of godly Christian teachers who are divinely gifted and called to teach and mold this impressionable age group.
- We pray for all of the social and emotional needs of our young students to be met. We pray that their hearts would be full of joy, and their elementary school experience would be uplifting despite the circumstances.
- Lord, please empower those little ones who fell behind developmentally, academically, or socially. Give them the skills and confidence they need to catch up to where they should be.
- Please bring alongside these students caring adults who can mentor and tutor them in areas where they are falling behind. Help the children know how loved and precious they are, and provide the specific tutoring they need to fill in any gaps.
- Pour out Your Spirit on these young ones, we pray! Let there be an awakening of their spirits and minds to You. May each student in America feel and see Your presence in their lives. May all of our children and the adults who teach and lead them encounter Your love and truth in a supernatural way!

WEEK 3: IGNITE SPIRITUAL AWAKENING ON CAMPUSES   81

Day 18: REVIVING MIDDLE SCHOOLS AND HIGH SCHOOLS

"Even a child makes himself known by his acts,
by whether his conduct is pure and upright."
(PROVERBS 20:11, ESV)

"Blessed are those whose way is blameless,
who walk in the law of the Lord!
Blessed are those who keep his testimonies,
who seek him with their whole heart,
who also do no wrong, but walk in his ways! You have
commanded your precepts to be kept diligently. Oh, that
my ways may be steadfast in keeping your statutes!"
(PSALM 119:1–5, ESV)

Middle school and high school can be an incredibly intense time for teens as they navigate friendship struggles, identity crises, bullying, and, especially in the high school years, dating, exposure to drugs, alcohol, sex, immense peer pressure, and much more. At the same time, their own bodies are changing rapidly, and as they navigate this confusing time, they are subject to mixed messaging everywhere they turn.

It's no wonder that almost 70 percent of Christian youth leave the Church after high school. It's one of the most volatile seasons of life for young people, and we must pray to cover our nation's middle schools and high schools with God's presence.

It's important for young people to know that "Christian life" can and does exist beyond chapels, church youth groups, and worship services—that their Christian values and beliefs are relevant in the world today. It is our deepest hope that the teens of America would discover the multitude of ways they can bring Christian life to their circles of friends and school campuses. Through Bible clubs, prayer groups, and being open about their faith with peers, high school students can become thriving catalysts for spiritual impact and transformation.

There are many ways teens can connect, communicate, and even gather to share and experience Christ together. We should be praying for boldness among the Christian teens in our communities, that they would bring more of their friends into the Kingdom of God on the mission field of their middle and high schools. These are crucial years for building character, values, and a vision for life.

At the same time, high school is ripe with temptation. There are daily spiritual battles taking place for our teens' purity, tempting them to believe that they must grow up sooner than they really should. We must stand against all forces that would tell them they need to drink, party, or sleep around in order to experience acceptance. We can pray, in Jesus' name, that all middle and high school students would discover their worth and wholeness in the eyes of Christ, and not in the eyes of the world or their peers.

We also need to be encouraging teens in their academic pursuits. Whether they choose to go on to college or advance to trade schools or apprenticeships, it is so important for them to place a value on their schooling and to diligently follow God's path to their chosen career. The last few years have presented a tornado of reasons for students to drop out of high school, and states and school districts are starting to see the fallout. At least thirty-one states saw declining graduation rates for the school year 2021—more than twice as many than in the previous year—with low-income students and those with disabilities being the hardest hit.[36]

---

36. Sarah D. Sparks, "Plunging Graduation Rates Signal Long Recovery," *Education Week*, August 29, 2022, Updated: August 30, 2022, https://www.edweek.org/teaching-learning/plunging-graduation-rates-signal-long-recovery/2022/08.

Our alternative high schools have unique student populations that are usually experiencing even higher levels of brokenness and challenges. Many times, these students are trying to overcome significant adversities and roadblocks to education and may be dealing with juvenile incarceration, housing insecurity, pregnancy and parenting, addictions, and more, in even greater numbers than in regular high schools. We need to remember these unique student and teacher populations as well.

Many students, whether they are in alternative or mainstream schools, fail to reach their full potential because they have no one to believe in them, encourage them, and pray for them. As the family of God, we can make a difference!

Let's Pray

- God, first and foremost, we pray for a great turnaround in the statistic that 70 percent of Christian youth leave the Church after high school. Heavenly Father, we ask You to intervene in our young people's lives and break this trend. Bring Your answers to parents, churches, and schools! In Jesus' name, keep our children close to You as they navigate the pressures of their teenage years.

- We pray for godly teachers, coaches, and school administrators to guide middle schoolers and high schoolers with truth and love.

- Among our students, we ask for edifying and fulfilling friendships rather than negative influences that would cause them to turn away from You.

- We pray You would give extra strength and grace to the teachers and administrators of alternative school students. On the students themselves, we pray You would pour out Your Spirit to help them overcome their adversity and go on to know You, follow You, and achieve success in their lives.

- We bind the spirits that lead teens into partying, substance abuse, and provocative behavior. Lord, surround our students with a hedge of Your protection. Cause them to feel a wholeness and acceptance that only comes from Your unfailing love.
- May the Christian students in all our middle and high schools walk in boldness, proudly proclaiming Your name. Anoint them with the bravery that only comes from You.
- We declare victory over all spirits that would bind our students in fear, preventing them from sharing openly about their faith. We pray against the fear of man, the fear of rejection, or any other trepidation that would make them feel anxious about sharing their testimony.
- May there be a wave of revival in our middle schools and high schools that sweeps across our state and our nation!

Day 19: BLESSING HOMESCHOOLS AND CHRISTIAN SCHOOLS

"You have been taught the Holy Scriptures from childhood, and they have given you the wisdom to receive the salvation that comes by trusting in Christ Jesus."
(2 TIMOTHY 3:15, NLT)

"God gave these four young men an unusual aptitude for understanding every aspect of literature and wisdom."
(DANIEL 1:17, NLT)

The history of Christian education in America has featured a broad range of schooling opportunities. Some of the early immigrants to this country came here in pursuit of religious freedom and soon founded community schooling options for children and adolescents.

Not too long after the European settlers moved to the New World, their desire to continue Christian education to the college and university level came to fruition. In fact, many of the oldest and most prestigious universities in this country were originally founded to provide Christian education and even training for Christian ministry. For centuries, Christian families have understood and appreciated the important values of Christian education.

There are many reasons why parents choose to send their children to private school or educate them at home. Many times, it is because they want to have greater opportunity to pursue a certain emphasis in their children's education. In some cases, children with special needs are not being served adequately by the local public school district. Others have been motivated to homeschool or send their children to a Christian school because they have become aware of the unprecedented assaults on truth and biblical values their children are facing in public school classrooms.

For these reasons and others, homeschooling rates within the United States are higher than they have been in decades. Between 2019 and 2021, homeschooling rates more than doubled.[37] Some families in the United States have created a modern version of the one-room schoolhouse, sometimes called "homeschooling pods." Under this model, a small group of parents split the cost of hiring teachers and tutors and paying for resources such as online classes.

Enrollment in Christian schools and universities is also on the rise. The national undergraduate enrollment rate at public universities dropped 1.1 percent during the fall 2022 semester and dropped an overall rate of 4.2 percent between 2020 and 2022, according to the National Student Clearinghouse Research Center. Many faith-based

---

37. "Homeschooling on the Rise During COVID-19 Pandemic," United States Census Bureau, March 22, 2021, https://www.census.gov/library/stories/2021/03/homeschooling-on-the-rise-during-covid-19-pandemic.html.

institutions, however, saw a notable increase in enrollment during this time.[38]

Whatever the reason parents may choose to utilize them, homeschools and private schools at all levels are extremely important components of our states' educational opportunities, and we want to pray for parents and teachers as they undertake this valuable endeavor. We also want to pray that states will continue to maintain options for school choice. Be alert to what is going on in your own state in this regard.

Let's Pray

- Lord, we thank You for every private Christian school, college, preschool, and godly homeschool in our state and nation. Thank you for the parents, teachers, and families who are hard at work educating the next generation in excellence and with a biblical worldview.
- As You did for Solomon and for Daniel, please give our Christian students maturity beyond their years and a supernatural ability to learn and to excel academically, above and beyond the norm.
- We invite Your manifest presence to come to these classrooms and homes, and we ask for a great move of God among these students, parents, and teachers! We pray for true revival to come to our Christian schools with a great outpouring of the Holy Spirit that would impact every family.
- We ask You, Jehovah Jireh, for a great financial blessing to come to each of these and pray that You would reward and bless them for their commitment and sacrifice: to the teacher

---

38. "Answered Prayer: Christian Schools See Increased Enrollment," Intercessors for America, January 11, 2023, https://ifapray.org/blog/christian -schools-see-increased-enrollment/.

in a Christian school with a significantly smaller paycheck, to the student paying tuition fees, and to the parent who experiences a loss of income to stay home and teach their children.

- Lord, please give wisdom and direction to the parents who are seeking You about whether they should choose homeschool or Christian school over public schools. We pray you would make available the finances, if that is a need, and give them Your assurance of provision for the choice they ultimately make.

- For those who choose homeschooling, we pray You would give them specific wisdom for each child this year, directing them to the concepts, content, and character qualities You want to be instilled in that child.

- We pray, Lord, that You would protect the right of parents to choose where their children go to school. We pray You would safeguard school choice and voucher systems that would enable parents to direct their tax dollars to schools of their choice.

- Many of our Christian schools and colleges face financial challenges, and we ask for dramatic financial breakthroughs for each of them! Protect these institutions from negative press designed to pressure them into compromising their stand for the gospel and righteousness. We pray for their governing boards to make decisions in the fear of the Lord and with great wisdom, and that You would guide them in the days ahead.

- Father, we fervently cry out to You for every Christian student, no matter their school or age. We ask that even our youngest Christian children would be taught Your truth from childhood and that they would have a deep understanding of the Bible. Please send them teachers and pastors who can impart an intelligent biblical worldview to them and disciple them into followers of You.

Day 20: AWAKENING COLLEGES AND UNIVERSITIES

"Oh, that you would rend the heavens and come
down, that the mountains would tremble before you!
As when fire sets twigs ablaze and causes water to
boil, come down to make your name known to your
enemies and cause nations to quake before you!"
(ISAIAH 64:1-2 NIV)

Today, college campuses serve a highly strategic purpose in the life of our nation. Not only are all of our nation's future leaders gathering to be trained and commissioned, but even the best and brightest from the nations of the world are being sent to our colleges and universities!

But there is a crisis on our college campuses today. They are in dire need of the presence of God! The reality is that many universities are not only training future leaders into occupational roles, they are also systematically shaping hearts and minds to have a worldview devoid of God. The effects have been devastating on a generation. The places that once trained young people in the Word of God are now the very places where most young people lose their faith.

The statistics support these observations: the emotional and mental health of college students has become a growing concern. According to a recent national survey, 95 percent of counseling center directors expressed increasing concern about the number of students "with significant psychological problems," and 70 percent indicated an increase in the number of students with severe psychological problems from the previous year.[39] Anxiety is the top presenting concern

---

39. "College Students' Mental Health a Growing Concern, Survey Finds," *American Psychological Association*, Vol 44, No. 6 (June 2013): 13.

(41.6 percent), followed by depression (36.3 percent) and relationship problems (35.8 percent).[40]

Additionally, according to Addiction Center, "College students make up one of the largest groups of drug abusers nationwide," and are "twice as likely to abuse drugs and alcohol than those who don't attend college."[41]

Yet, in similar times in our nation's history, when darkness has overtaken our colleges and universities, and when God's people have united in faith to pray for the outpouring of God's Spirit on colleges, He has responded to reclaim a generation!

As I was writing Day 20, an outpouring of the Holy Spirit took place at Asbury University, a private Christian school in Wilmore, Kentucky. What started as a routine chapel service broke out in ongoing worship and passion for Christ led by the students: heartfelt contrition and repentance of sin; the obvious lingering presence of the Holy Spirit; and a hunger for His Word. Classes were canceled for a number of days and people flooded into Wilmore from across the nation and around the world. Even as open meetings wound down at Asbury, other campuses began to experience this palpable presence of God, too.

Let's continue to pray that God will release His revival flood on colleges and universities all across the nation and that the fire will spread to homes, churches, and the nation at large.

40. Margarita Tartakovsky, "Depression and Anxiety Among College Students," *Psych Central*, October 8, 2018, Updated on April 12, 2022, https://psychcentral.com/lib/depression-and-anxiety-among-college-students.
41. Jeffrey Juergens, "College Students and Drug Abuse," *Addiction Center*, October 26, 2022, https://www.addictioncenter.com/college.

Let's Pray

- Father, we pray today for our colleges and universities, that they would be filled with Your tangible presence.
- Lord, we pray for a movement of holiness, righteousness, and purity on the college campuses of America that will cause the student body to be washed clean by the blood of Jesus (see Heb. 9:14; 1 John 1:7)! We pray for a revelation of the beauty of Your holiness (see Ps. 27:4, 29:2). We pray that they would desire to seek You and honor You above all, to turn away from all sin, and to be holy as You are holy (see 1 Pet. 1:15–16).
- Lord, we ask You to break off every addiction to alcohol, drugs, pornography, and sexual immorality among the student body and the faculty. We ask for the power of Your Spirit within hearts to renounce all agreements with destructive lifestyles and sin patterns, and to find complete freedom, cleansing, and healing by the blood of Jesus!
- Lord, we pray each student will have the opportunity to grow and develop spiritually as well as intellectually, and that they would be grounded in the truth.
- We thank You for those students who are courageously living out their faith and displaying it on campus. Give our Christian students courage to stand strong in an atmosphere that is often antagonistic to faith.
- Lord, we lift up the professors, deans, and presidents of our colleges. We ask that they would not only be wise in their area of specialty, but also that You would give them spiritual wisdom. We pray Your Holy Spirit will use Christian professors and faculty as a mighty force for truth, and that a new standard of righteousness will be raised up on our campuses.
- We ask for an all-consuming hunger and desperation for Your presence on our college and university campuses that only You

can give—that students would desire You more than anything else in this life! Let nothing else satisfy them but the presence of God, touching an entire generation!

- Lord, we know that many spiritual awakenings have started on college and university campuses, and we ask You to do it again. We pray You would ignite the fires of revival on university campuses all across our nation, releasing a holy cleansing flood of Your presence and power that will sweep millions of young people into Your Kingdom.

Day 21: RECLAIM A GENERATION

". . . that they may be called oaks of righteousness,
the planting of the LORD, that he may be glorified.
They shall build up the ancient ruins;
they shall raise up the former devastations;
they shall repair the ruined cities,
the devastations of many generations."
(ISAIAH 61:3–4, ESV)

If we are to see revival in our day and reformation in our lifetime, we must influence and reform the educational systems of our nation. A generation has very nearly been stolen from us, and it must be reclaimed for the Kingdom of God. We need an invasion of prayer power and reformers into every facet of society if we are to see transformation and a great reformation occur!

Daniel and his friends Shadrach, Meshach, and Abednego were all young Hebrew men of excellence, trained in the ways of the Babylonians (see Dan. 1:3–4). They took their Hebrew heritage and applied it, without compromise, to their pagan surroundings. They were not distracted by the attractions and temptations of the affluent culture they found themselves in. Anointed and appointed by God, they experienced supernatural intervention and changed the course of a nation.

We need a godly generation to arise in our day, equipped and skilled in ways our culture will listen and respond to. This will be no simple task. While Christian influence in our school systems has been all but eradicated, secular humanists have been discipling our children into their belief system. Through their calculated efforts over many decades, humanists and atheists have commandeered our education system and used it to propagate their ideologies. As a result, as we have spoken about throughout this prayer guide, a dark and evil anti-Christ force is currently dominating our school systems.

Yet we are not without hope! God's Word is full of promises for the children and grandchildren of the righteous. He has a plan for this generation and He will fulfill it! Together, let's declare His Word over our children. It will not return to Him void:

> "This is what the LORD says: 'Restrain your voice from weeping and your eyes from tears, for your work will be rewarded,' declares the LORD. 'They [your children] will return from the land of the enemy. So there is hope for your descendants,' declares the LORD." (Jer. 31:16–17, NIV)

> "Be assured, an evil person will not go unpunished, but the offspring of the righteous will be delivered." (Prov. 11:21, ESV)

> "And all your [spiritual] children shall be disciples [taught by the Lord and obedient to His will], and great shall be the peace and undisturbed composure of your children." (Isa. 54:13, AMPC)

> "Blessed are those who fear the LORD, who find great delight in his commands. Their children will be mighty in the land; the generation of the upright will be blessed." (Psalm 112:1–2, NIV)

"For I will pour water on the thirsty land, and streams on the dry ground; I will pour out my Spirit on your offspring, and my blessing on your descendants." (Isa. 44:3, NIV)

"For thus says the LORD: 'Even the captives of the mighty shall be taken, and the prey of the tyrant be rescued, for I will contend with those who contend with you, and I will save your children.'" (Isa. 49:25, ESV)

For good or evil, the education system is a training ground for our young people. We cannot be silent or passive; we must get involved with our prayers and godly actions. If we are to see revival and reformation in our nation, we must raise up and equip a generation of young people like Daniel and his friends. We must claim the promises of God for the next generation and pray He raises them up as reformers and world-changers!

Let's Pray

- Father, we praise You that You have heard every prayer during these past 21 days as we have cried out to You on behalf of our students, teachers, families, and schools. We ask that You would be glorified. Be exalted over our schools and over every power and principality that would seek to influence and infiltrate our education system with the purpose to deceive and destroy the next generation.
- We ask You to bless the students in preschools, homeschools, alternative, private, charter, and public schools, and colleges and universities of America with the Spirit of wisdom and revelation in the knowledge of You, Your Word, and Your Kingdom purposes.
- We declare it is time for our Christian students and teachers to *arise*. As Your glory rises upon them, we declare that

the nations will come to the brightness of Your rising (see Isa. 60:1,3).

- Almighty God, we pray for our future leaders. Raise up young people with godly purpose and destiny to contend for the future of our nation! May many great young leaders arise from our schools to bring justice and truth to every sector of society.
- Raise up those who will lead the way for truth in every sphere of influence: in government, education, media, entertainment, the arts, business and finance, science and technology, families, and the Church. May they fulfill the purpose of God in their generation. Like David, may they know their callings from a young age, that no amount of family negativity, peer pressure, or setbacks would discourage them from pursuing them. We declare they will walk in Your plan for them, a plan that leads to life and fullness of joy.
- Reveal Yourself and Your ways in undeniable and sovereign acts. Empower and equip our children to fulfill their sovereign purpose according to the highest plans of God, in Jesus' name.
- May thousands of young leaders spring up from across our nation—students who are wise beyond their years, faithful to the truth, and effective apologists for the gospel. Release the fivefold ministry (see Eph. 4:11) in our schools, we pray. Raise up leaders, pastors, teachers, prophets, and evangelists!

APPENDIX

PRAYERS OF DEDICATION AND DECLARATION FOR YOUR SCHOOL

Whether you are a parent, grandparent, student, teacher, principal, school administrator, or concerned citizen, we encourage you to make this prayer your own. Personalize these powerful prayers by inserting the name of the school(s) you are praying for. In the Student's Prayer of Personal Surrender, you may want to insert the name of your child, grandchild, or a student you care about, and stand in the gap for them.

I dedicate _____ school, its campus, the buildings, the students, and the faculty to Your purposes, God. I firmly declare that Jesus Christ is Lord over this school and there is no other God over _____ school, but You. I invite Your Holy Spirit to rule and reign over the campus now and for the entire school year. I declare that the peace and presence of God will permeate the halls, classrooms, library, sports fields, gymnasium, offices, and every building on this campus.

May the atmosphere of _____ school be permeated with Your spirit of salvation, repentance, revival, and renewal for every student, teacher, principal, parent, and worker now and every day throughout the school year.

I dedicate this school as a place of safety with an environment conducive to learning and growing in godly character. From this place may leaders like Moses, Joshua, Joseph, Daniel, Ruth, and Esther arise, going into all sectors of society to contend for truth and justice.

Praying Biblical Declarations Over the Campus

- Lord, shine Your light upon _____ school and drive out all darkness [spiritual blindness, perversion of truth, and hostilities toward You] (see Eph. 6:18-20).
- I declare that by the power of Jesus Christ this campus is a suicide-, drug-, and promiscuity-free zone! Spirits of death, depression, oppression, and hopelessness have no place on this campus, in Jesus' name. I declare that students will be filled with God's life and truth and will walk in His ways (see Col. 1:13).
- Mighty God, in Jesus' name, I declare that ungodly gangs, crime, violence, and all other illegal activities will have no place within the boundaries of this school or this neighborhood (see Isa. 60:18).
- Father God, be exalted in _____ school. Release Your salvation to permeate every person that comes upon the campus (see Matt. 9:37-38). Raise up strong and godly leadership among clubs on this campus. Bless Christian prayer on the _____ campus and cause Your Kingdom to be advanced in and through it! I declare that doors of opportunity are opening to creatively share the gospel and that multitudes will be saved (see 1 Cor. 16:9; Eph. 6:18-20).

A Student's Prayer of Personal Surrender

Father, I know that You have given me a call to influence my school and I accept it as my mission field. I receive that call with gratitude and a sense of responsibility. You have plans for this school and I believe You have plans for me. Help me to see my friends, my peers, those younger than me and those older than me, my teachers, and the school administrators through Your eyes. Give me courage to step out in the ways You are calling me to step out. Give me the strength to keep my heart and mind pure, focused on You above all the noise of the day-to-day circumstances, trials, and temptations. I now avail myself to Your greater purposes and plans for me, my school, and my sphere of influence.

WAYS TO ENGAGE
THE CHURCH COMMUNITY

Although there are so many issues that are plaguing our schools and our youth, we believe God is the solution to the most difficult of problems and wants to intervene in response to His people's prayers.

We encourage you to invite churches, families, youth groups, children's churches, and individuals to pray with you in an intentional and focused way as you lift up schools in your community to God. Select a specific 21-day time period and make available this *Reclaim a Generation* prayer guide to equip you and your group or congregation to pray effectively.

Ways to Engage Everyone

Select one or more schools that God lays on your heart. Set aside time to pray specifically for that school, its issues, students, teachers, administrators, and district leaders. We HIGHLY encourage you to prayerwalk or prayer drive several times a week around the perimeter of your chosen school. Prayerwalking or prayer driving near and around a school helps engage hearts to pray with more fervency and focus for the needs of the teachers and students.

Pastors/Churches

If you are a pastor or church leader, consider setting aside a weekend service to honor and pray for educators (especially effective near the time the school year starts in the fall). Ask God's blessing over them and pray for empowerment to succeed and prosper throughout the school year.

Encourage your congregation to pray together as families for their children's schools. Create a special service to pray for all the schools in your area. Make it a time to pray for their young people, educators, and the school year as a whole. This could be a churchwide prayer meeting with every age participating.

Select the nearest school or school district and pray for its principals and key leadership by name during the weekend service. Consider having church members form small groups to pray together. On a Saturday during the 21 days, you could organize multiple churchwide prayerwalks near different school locations and set up coordinators for each prayerwalking team.

Youth Groups/Youth Pastors

Youth groups and youth pastors can set aside time at each of their youth services to pray for a different topic related to schools (friends by name, activities and clubs, their school leadership/administration, etc.) They could organize prayerwalks around the perimeter of the students' schools one Saturday, engaging the whole youth group to target different schools together.

TIPS FOR SCHOOL PRAYERWALKING

What is prayerwalking? Prayerwalking is talking with our Heavenly Father through His Son Jesus Christ while walking. Here, our focus is upon our neighborhood schools.

Praying near a campus brings us in close proximity with our prayer target. We begin to see with the eyes and compassion of Jesus the needs of the young people for whom we are interceding.

Three components work together while prayerwalking:

1. **Worship.** Proclaim the excellencies of the name of Jesus or softly sing a song which exalts the Lord and His mighty power.
2. **Welcome.** Invite God's transforming presence to permeate the school for which you are praying.
3. **Warfare.** Prayerwalking is spiritual battle. You may experience an indirect onslaught of the enemy: confusion or pestering of the mind, causing your thoughts to wander, or telling you this isn't doing any good. Press through these roadblocks. Realize that the Lord has given you authority over the evil one. Remember that in every place you walk, you have been given spiritual authority to restrain, limit, and displace evil forces (Josh. 1:3; Luke 10:19).

Integrate these three "Ws" in a good balance, though at times you may sense that you need to emphasize one more than another.

Do's and Don'ts of Prayerwalking

Do: Worship God as you prayerwalk or prayer drive the school's perimeter. Welcome God's Holy Spirit to the school for which you are praying. Pronounce blessings upon the teachers, students, and staff. Pray salvation, healing, and spiritual freedom for the students who attend there.

Don't: Draw attention to yourself. You have an audience of One—Jesus Christ. It would be best not to go on the campus during school hours since there is increased security at schools these days (go before or after school or on weekends).

In Preparation

It is important to prepare your mind, body, and spirit. You are about to become a bridge of blessing between Heaven and earth! Don't allow any feelings of inadequacy to plague you. You have indicated your willingness by your presence, and God is always faithful to take us where we are and lead us. In prayer, there is no failure.

The book *Prayerwalking,* by Steve Hawthorne and Graham Kendrick, offers the following tips to prepare for a prayerwalk:

1. Start with vocalizing your praise to the Lord. Whether you sing, shout, or whisper, warm up your vocal cords with praise before setting out. Put the name of Jesus on your lips.
2. Seek to position your heart before God in fresh gratitude and blessing.
3. Take charge of the directions your mind will go.
4. Fix your attention on the purposes and ways and thoughts of God before you launch out. If you find your mind wandering, read Scripture out loud.
5. Seek God for guidance at intervals. Then trust that He is guiding you!

Tips for School Prayerwalking

- Take a few minutes to connect and pray with others on your prayer team. Find out if anyone is sensing/hearing anything from the Lord.
- Take your stance before the Father. Remember that you are positioned in heavenly places through the blood and authority of Jesus.

What to Do During the Prayerwalk

1. Open your eyes. Ask God to help you see with His eyes.
2. Open your ears. Listen for God's whispered cues. Expect Him to highlight truths you have hidden in your heart and apply them to what is around you. Practice silence as you listen to God's Spirit.
3. Pray together. Seek to consciously follow and reinforce prayers lifted by others on the prayer team.
4. Pray with Scripture. You can be confident of praying the will of God when you are praying His Word. God has breathed life into His Word and loves to bless it. He has promised that His Word will not return to Him void. Read it over and over again.
5. Pray with Holy Spirit sensitivity to the people and places you are actually encountering. Don't be surprised if the Lord guides you to focus and concentrate your prayers on some locations more than others.

What to Pray

Based on the Lord's Prayer: *"He said to them, 'When you pray, say: "Father, hallowed be your name, your kingdom come. Give us each day our daily bread. Forgive us our sins, for we also forgive everyone who sins against us. And lead us not into temptation.""* (Luke 11:2-4, NIV).

1. Pray for God's glory. Pray that God will work in such a way that He will be honored, adored, lifted up, revealed, and praised by name among our students and in our schools.
2. Pray for God's Kingdom. Pray with expectancy for Heaven's liberating power to be released on the students and schools.
3. Pray for reconciliation. Ask God to reconcile every student to Himself. Ask God to bring reconciliation where there are offenses or breaches among students themselves, and between students and teachers.
4. Pray for God to release His Spirit on the campus. Pray He would lead all students, teachers, administrators, and support staff into the light of His love and truth, rescuing them from darkness and destruction and reclaiming them for the purposes of Heaven.

Scriptures for Prayerwalking

(Note: All scriptures are from the NIV version.)

"Shout for joy to God, all the earth! Sing the glory of his name; make his praise glorious. How awesome are your deeds! So great is your power that your enemies cringe before you. All the earth bows down to you; they sing praise to you, they sing the praises of your name" (Psalm 66:1–4).

"And they were calling to one another: 'Holy, holy, holy is the Lord Almighty; the whole earth is full of his glory.'" (Isaiah 6:3).

"May God be gracious to us and bless us and make his face shine on us so that your ways may be known on earth, your salvation among all nations. May the peoples praise you, God; may all the peoples praise you" (Psalm 67:1–3).

"A voice of one calling: 'In the wilderness prepare the way for the Lord; make straight in the desert a highway for our God. Every

valley shall be raised up, every mountain and hill made low; the rough ground shall become level, the rugged places a plain. And the glory of the Lord will be revealed, and all people will see it together. For the mouth of the Lord has spoken"' (Isaiah 40:3-5).

"Let this be written for a future generation, that a people not yet created may praise the Lord: 'The Lord looked down from his sanctuary on high, from heaven he viewed the earth, to hear the groans of the prisoners and release those condemned to death"' (Psalm 102:18-20).

"Rather, as it is written: 'Those who were not told about him will see, and those who have not heard will understand"' (Romans 15:21.)

"Teach me your way, Lord, that I may rely on your faithfulness; give me an undivided heart, that I may fear your name. I will praise you, Lord my God, with all my heart; I will glorify your name forever. For great is your love toward me; you have delivered me from the depths, from the realm of the dead" (Psalm 86:11-13.

"When you pray, say: 'Father, hallowed be your name, your kingdom come. Give us each day our daily bread. Forgive us our sins, for we also forgive everyone who sins against us. And lead us not into temptation"' (Luke 11:2-4).

"I urge, then, first of all, that petitions, prayers, intercession, and thanksgiving be made for all people, for kings and all those in authority, that we may live peaceful and quiet lives in all godliness and holiness. This is good, and pleases God our Savior, who wants all people to be saved and to come to a knowledge of the truth" (1 Timothy 2:1-4).

"He told them, 'The harvest is plentiful, but the workers are few. Ask the Lord of the harvest, therefore, to send out workers into his harvest field"' (Luke 10:2).

RESOURCES

For parents:

Prayer Saturated Schools—is a ministry of BridgeBuilders International, led by Hal and Cheryl Sacks. The BridgeBuilders' team empowers more than 5 million Christians—including pastors, law enforcement, and legislators—to invite God's transforming presence into every cultural sphere of influence (see 2 Chron. 7:14). They provide resources to help you pray for students, their schools, and the education system.
PrayerSaturated.school
BridgeBuilders.net

Moms for Liberty—is dedicated to fighting for the survival of America by unifying, educating, and empowering parents to defend their parental rights at all levels of government.
MomsforLiberty.org

WallBuilders—is an organization dedicated to presenting America's forgotten history and heroes, with an emphasis on the moral, religious, and constitutional foundation on which America was built—a foundation which, in recent years, has been seriously attacked and undermined.
WallBuilders.com

For Christian educators:

Christian Educators—Christian Educators is a professional association that supports, connects, and protects Christians working in our public schools, so they can be thriving ambassadors for Christ. As an alternative to politicized teachers' unions, Christian Educators supports Christian teachers from a biblical worldview and does not spend membership dues on politically driven agendas and issues.

There are many free resources for teachers at its website and there is also a membership available that includes liability insurance, job protection benefits to provide for a local attorney, and unlimited educational and legal consultations with experts.

Access these resources and learn more at ChristianEducators. org, or reach out at 888-798-1124 or info@christianeducators.org.

Rise Up Summit—An annual free online conference that equips educators from both public and private schools with practical and spiritual sessions and tools.
RiseUpChristianEducators.com

Gateways to Better Education—A nonprofit organization founded in 1991 to help public school educators, parents, and school leaders foster faith-welcoming schools as well as teach about the Bible and Christianity without mixing church and state.
GoGateways.org

ABOUT THE AUTHOR

CHERYL SACKS is a best-selling author, national conference speaker, prayer mobilizer, and church prayer consultant. Her "Prayer Saturated" series—including *The Prayer Saturated Church* (NavPress/Tyndale), *Prayer Saturated Kids* (NavPress/Tyndale), and *The Prayer Saturated Family* (Chosen)—have blessed and mentored tens of thousands of individuals to go deeper into prayer. Her newly released book, *Fire on the Family Altar* (Destiny Image), is a handbook to equip families to invite the power of the Holy Spirit into their homes to bring healing and transformation.

A former public schoolteacher and administrator, Cheryl's heart is to see a new generation of youth empowered to pray with purpose and passion and to become reformers for the Kingdom of God in their spheres of influence. Cheryl and her husband, Hal, lead Bridge-Builders International based in Phoenix, Arizona. They have a married daughter and three grandchildren.

Learn more about Hal and Cheryl Sacks' ministry at:
prayersaturated.life
bridgebuilders.net

PRAISE FOR JU

MW00577043

THE BEACH H_____ ___

"Love the characters in this series. This series was my first introduction to Judith Keim. She is now one of my favorites. Looking forward to reading more of her books."

BREAKFAST AT THE BEACH HOUSE HOTEL *is an easy, delightful read that offers romance, family relationships, and strong women learning to be stronger. Real life situations filter through the pages. Enjoy!"*

LUNCH AT THE BEACH HOUSE HOTEL *– "This series is such a joy to read. You feel you are actually living with them. Can't wait to read the latest one."*

DINNER AT THE BEACH HOUSE HOTEL *– "A Terrific Read! As usual, Judith Keim did it again. Enjoyed immensely. Continue writing such pleasantly reading books for all of us readers."*

CHRISTMAS AT THE BEACH HOUSE HOTEL *– "Not Just Another Christmas Novel. This is book number four in the series and my introduction to Judith Keim's writing. I wasn't disappointed. The characters are dimensional and engaging. The plot is well crafted and advances at a pleasing pace. The Florida location is interesting and warming. It was a delight to read a romance novel with mature female protagonists. Ann and Rhoda have life experiences that enrich the story. It's a clever book about friends and extended family. Buy copies for your book group pals and enjoy this seasonal read."*

MARGARITAS AT THE BEACH HOUSE HOTEL *– "What a wonderful series. I absolutely loved this book and can't wait for the next book to come out. There was even suspense in it. Thanks Judith for the great stories."*

i

"Overall, *Margaritas at the Beach House Hotel* is another wonderful addition to the series. Judith Keim takes the reader on a journey told through the voices of these amazing characters we have all come to love through the years! I truly cannot stress enough how good this book is, and I hope you enjoy it as much as I have!"

THE HARTWELL WOMEN SERIES – Books 1 – 4

"This was an EXCELLENT series. When I discovered Judith Keim, I read all of her books back to back. I thoroughly enjoyed the women Keim has written about. They are believable and you want to just jump into their lives and be their friends! I can't wait for any upcoming books!"

"I fell into Judith Keim's Hartwell Women series and have read & enjoyed all of her books in every series. Each centers around a strong & interesting woman character and their family interaction. Good reads that leave you wanting more."

THE FAT FRIDAYS GROUP – Books 1 – 3

"Excellent story line for each character, and an insightful representation of situations which deal with some of the contemporary issues women are faced with today."

"I love this author's books. Her characters and their lives are realistic. The power of women's friendships is a common and beautiful theme that is threaded throughout this story."

THE SALTY KEY INN SERIES – Books 1 – 4

FINDING ME – "I thoroughly enjoyed the first book in this series and cannot wait for the others! The characters are endearing with the same struggles we all encounter. The setting makes me feel like I am a guest at The Salty Key

Inn...relaxed, happy & light-hearted! The men are yummy and the women strong. You can't get better than that! Happy Reading!"

FINDING MY WAY- "Loved the family dynamics as well as uncertain emotions of dating and falling in love. Appreciated the morals and strength of parenting throughout. Just couldn't put this book down."

FINDING LOVE – "I waited for this book because the first two was such good reads. This one didn't disappoint.... Judith Keim always puts substance into her books. This book was no different, I learned about PTSD, accepting oneself, there is always going to be problems but stick it out and make it work. Just the way life is. In some ways a lot like my life. Judith is right, it needs another book and I will definitely be reading it. Hope you choose to read this series, you will get so much out of it."

FINDING FAMILY – "Completing this series is like eating the last chip. Love Judith's writing, and her female characters are always smart, strong, vulnerable to life and love experiences."

"This was a refreshing book. Bringing the heart and soul of the family to us."

CHANDLER HILL INN SERIES – Books 1 – 3

GOING HOME – "I absolutely could not put this book down. Started at night and read late into the middle of the night. As a child of the '60s, the Vietnam war was front and center so this resonated with me. All the characters in the book were so well developed that the reader felt like they were friends of the family."

"I was completely immersed in this book, with the beautiful descriptive writing, and the authors' way of bringing her characters to life. I felt like I was right inside her story."

COMING HOME – "Coming Home is a winner. The characters are well-developed, nuanced and likable. Enjoyed the vineyard setting, learning about wine growing and seeing the challenges Cami faces in running and growing a business. I look forward to the next book in this series!"

"Coming Home was such a wonderful story. The author has such a gift for getting the reader right to the heart of things."

HOME AT LAST – "In this wonderful conclusion, to a heartfelt and emotional trilogy set in Oregon's stunning wine country, Judith Keim has tied up the Chandler Hill series with the perfect bow."

"Overall, this is truly a wonderful addition to the Chandler Hill Inn series. Judith Keim definitely knows how to perfectly weave together a beautiful and heartfelt story."

"The storyline has some beautiful scenes along with family drama. Judith Keim has created characters with interactions that are believable and some of the subjects the story deals with are poignant."

SEASHELL COTTAGE BOOKS

A CHRISTMAS STAR – "Love, laughter, sadness, great food, and hope for the future, all in one book. It doesn't get any better than this stunning read."

"A Christmas Star is a heartwarming Christmas story featuring endearing characters. So many Christmas books are set in snowbound places...it was a nice change to read a Christmas story that takes place on a warm sandy beach!" Susan Peterson

CHANGE OF HEART – "CHANGE OF HEART is the

summer read we've all been waiting for. Judith Keim is a master at creating fascinating characters that are simply irresistible. Her stories leave you with a big smile on your face and a heart bursting with love."

~Kellie Coates Gilbert, author of the popular Sun Valley Series

A SUMMER OF SURPRISES – "The story is filled with a roller coaster of emotions and self-discovery. Finding love again and rebuilding family relationships."

"Ms. Keim uses this book as an amazing platform to show that with hard emotional work, belief in yourself and love, the scars of abuse can be conquered. It in no way preaches, it's a lovely story with a happy ending."

"The character development was excellent. I felt I knew these people my whole life. The story development was very well thought out I was drawn [in] from the beginning."

A ROAD TRIP TO REMEMBER – "I LOVED this book! Love the character development, the fun, the challenges and the ending. My favorite books are about strong, competent women finding their own path to success and happiness and this is a winner. It's one of those books you just can't put down."

"The characters are so real that they jump off the page. Such a fun, HAPPY book at the perfect time. It will lift your spirits and even remind you of your own grandmother. Spirited and hopeful Aggie gets a second chance at love and she takes the steering wheel and drives straight for it."

THE DESERT SAGE INN SERIES – Books 1 – 4

THE DESERT FLOWERS – ROSE – "The Desert Flowers - Rose, is the first book in the new series by Judith Keim. I always look forward to new books by Judith Keim, and this one is definitely a wonderful way to begin The Desert Sage Inn Series!"

"In this first of a series, we see each woman come into her own and view new beginnings even as they must take this tearful journey as they slowly lose a dear friend. This is a very well written book with well-developed and likable main characters. It was interesting and enlightening as the first portion of this saga unfolded. I very much enjoyed this book and I do recommend it"

"Judith Keim is one of those authors that you can always depend on to give you a great story with fantastic characters. I'm excited to know that she is writing a new series and after reading book 1 in the series, I can't wait to read the rest of the books."!

THE DESERT FLOWERS – LILY – "The second book in the Desert Flowers series is just as wonderful as the first. Judith Keim is a brilliant storyteller. Her characters are truly lovely and people that you want to be friends with as soon as you start reading. Judith Keim is not afraid to weave real life conflict and loss into her stories. I loved reading Lily's story and can't wait for Willow's!

"The Desert Flowers Lily is the second book in The Desert Sage Inn Series by author Judith Keim. When I read the first book in the series, The Desert Flowers-Rose, I knew this series would exceed all of my expectations and then some. Judith Keim is an amazing author, and this series is a testament to her writing skills and her ability to completely draw a reader into the world of her characters."

CHRISTMAS JOY

SOUL SISTERS AT CEDAR MOUNTAIN LODGE, BOOK 12

JUDITH KEIM

CHRISTMAS JOY Copyright © 2022 by Judith Keim
All rights reserved. No part of CHRISTMAS JOY may be reproduced or transmitted in any form or by any means, electronic or mechanical including photocopying, recording, or by any information storage and retrieval system without the written permission of the author, except for the use of brief quotations in a book review. For permissions contact the author directly via electronic mail:
wildquail.pub@gmail.com
www.judithkeim.com

Published in the United States of America by:
Wild Quail Publishing
P.O. Box 171332
Boise, ID 83717-1332

ISBN # **978-1-954325-57-9**
FIRST EDITION

Dedication

This book is dedicated to women everywhere who reach out a
helping hand to spread joy to others in small ways and big –
Sisters of the Heart

BOOKS BY JUDITH KEIM

THE HARTWELL WOMEN SERIES:

The Talking Tree – 1

Sweet Talk – 2

Straight Talk – 3

Baby Talk – 4

The Hartwell Women – Boxed Set

THE BEACH HOUSE HOTEL SERIES:

Breakfast at The Beach House Hotel – 1

Lunch at The Beach House Hotel – 2

Dinner at The Beach House Hotel – 3

Christmas at The Beach House Hotel – 4

Margaritas at The Beach House Hotel – 5

Dessert at The Beach House Hotel – 6

THE FAT FRIDAYS GROUP:

Fat Fridays – 1

Sassy Saturdays – 2

Secret Sundays – 3

THE SALTY KEY INN SERIES:

SEASHELL COTTAGE BOOKS:

THE CHANDLER HILL INN SERIES:

THE DESERT SAGE INN SERIES:

The Desert Flowers – Mistletoe & Holly – 4 (2022)

SOUL SISTERS AT CEDAR MOUNTAIN LODGE:

Christmas Sisters – Anthology

Christmas Kisses

Christmas Castles

Christmas Joy – (2022)

THE SANDERLING COVE INN SERIES:

Waves of Hope – (2022)

Sandy Wishes – (2023)

Salty Kisses – (2023)

OTHER BOOKS:

The ABC's of Living With a Dachshund

Once Upon a Friendship – Anthology

Winning BIG – a little love story for all ages

Holiday Hopes

The Winning Tickets – (2023)

For more information: **www.judithkeim.com**

CHAPTER 1

On this early Fall morning, Hailey Kirby Hensley walked along the white sand of the beach in front of the house she and her husband, Nick, owned along the Gulf Coast of Florida, observing her children at play. More than four years had passed since Brady and Luna had entered their lives. Nine now, Brady was a tall, healthy boy with auburn hair and brown eyes, who'd no doubt inherited his sturdy body from his father, Mac MacGrath, a famous football star. His four-year-old sister, Luna, was an athletic girl with shiny brown hair and green eyes like her mother, Linnie. Luna loved to build sandcastles with her younger sister, April. At three, April looked like Hailey with strawberry-blond hair and blue eyes, and though she was dainty, she managed to keep up with the others through sheer determination.

Hailey's eyes rested on the girls. Standing side by side, holding hands as they faced the water, Luna and April reminded her of her sister, Alissa, and herself. A pang of regret swept through her. She sometimes wished she wasn't so far away from her adoptive mother and three soul sisters. Especially Alissa.

Brady sprinted along the sand by her, chased by Zeke, their black and tan dachshund, and Tiger, the little white fluffy dog a woman had given Hailey one day on the beach just before Hailey discovered she was pregnant with April.

Filled with joy at the memory, Hailey thought back to that time …

She could still see the shock on Alissa's face and feel the same shock roaring through her own body when they realized they were both pregnant during their special girl's weekend that April four years ago. Though she was bursting with the news, Hailey had waited to tell Nick until after Alissa returned to her home in Granite Ridge, Idaho. Then, as soon as Brady and Luna were settled in bed, she'd approached him, her pulse fluttering with excitement and a bit of nerves, too.

Stretched out on the couch, looking as exhausted as he'd claimed to be, Nick took hold of her hand. "I don't know how you do it, Hailey. It's been only a couple of days taking care of Brady and Luna, and even with some help, I could sleep for a week. Good thing we're not worrying about any more kids for the time being, huh?"

Hailey took a seat on the couch beside him, bit her lip, and nodded.

Nick reached up and cupped a hand to her cheek. "Hey, what's wrong?"

"Nothing exactly. In fact, I have wonderful news." Her eyes had filled with tears at the thought that he might not be ready for this after the shock of being left with Brady and Luna.

He sat up and put his arm around her. "What is it? You can tell me."

She lifted her face to his. "Nick, you and I are going to have a baby!"

"Wait! Another baby?" A look of confusion crossed his face.

She nodded. "I know it's a surprise, and you didn't want to think of more children, but ..."

His expression morphed from confusion to pure joy. "A baby? Us? That's great! When?"

"Sometime next fall, around Thanksgiving, I'm guessing." Her voice wobbled. "Will you be ready?"

He hugged her tight. "I'll be such a professional father by then you won't believe it. Hailey, I love you. Aren't you as excited as I am?"

She took a moment to respond. Luna was just over three months old. Brady was becoming more involved with pre-school and friends, taking more and more of her attention. At the same time, she was starting another "Charlie and Zeke" book with a firm deadline. But when she saw the glow of happiness on Nick's face, all worries about handling another baby disappeared. They'd raise all their children together, like they'd promised one another.

As they got used to the idea, their happiness grew even deeper. Even Zeke and Tiger seemed to know something had changed, and in the mornings when Hailey wasn't feeling well, they stayed by her side. The rest of the time, they were with either Luna or Brady protecting them as always.

"All of this is excellent material for your new book," her agent declared while checking on her progress. Hailey had thought the seashore book was her best, but she was pretty sure the "Charlie welcomes a baby sister book" was going to be even better.

Brady became more and more interested in the idea of having a new baby in the house after seeing Hailey's stomach expand.

When they found out they were going to have a sister for Luna and Brady, Nick and Hailey studied girl names. Brady announced he liked the name April the best, and they agreed with him. That was the name of the special month that would always mean so much to them.

After a difficult delivery, April arrived in early November, and they'd spent another Christmas with a newborn, along with a toddler, and a grown-up five-year-old who spent a lot of time with Nick doing "guy stuff."

That Christmas, Nick pulled her aside. "I love you, Hailey, as my wife and the mother of my children. Maybe we can get away for a weekend to celebrate Valentine's Day."

Hailey glanced at him wide-eyed. "Valentine's Day? Oh, Nick, after what happened last time, I'm not ready to add another baby to our special castles."

Nick laughed. "Maybe we'd better wait for a year or two and just have a romantic dinner."

"That sounds better." Hailey hugged him. Though their lives had been turned upside down, their growing family was everything she and Nick had always wanted.

Now, watching her children, she knew she was right. Three children were perfect for them. Each was unique, requiring different things from her, and she wanted the time to do everything she could for them. They gave her such joy.

April was already showing signs of being artistic. And much to their surprise, Brady had musical talent and a lovely singing voice. He and Nick loved to play music together and were going to take part in a local talent contest for the fun of it. Luna was quick-witted and kept them active.

"Mommy! Come look at our cassel," April said.

While waiting for Hailey to cross the sand to her, Luna did her version of a cartwheel. She was a physically active child who was well-coordinated. No doubt, she'd be a gymnast like she wanted. She was a strong-minded little girl.

Hailey examined the castle the children had made out of buckets full of sand. From an early age, her children knew how special sandcastles were to her. For Hailey, they represented homes and places where everyone could feel comfortable. She'd used the sandcastle idea to help Brady understand that with both his parents deceased, he had a new home with Nick and her. It was something he could understand, and while grieving for his parents, he was comfortable and happy with his new surroundings.

What a time that had been. Luna was a newborn

5

when that fateful automobile accident had happened to Linnie and Mac, so she had no memories of her birth parents. But Hailey made sure she knew about them. Even now, stick figures inside the castle sometimes included them.

"This is a beautiful castle," said Hailey, studying their work. She could clearly see the difference between Luna's more sophisticated contribution and April's artistic additions. But she loved both versions. "Do you have a story to tell with this one?"

As an author and illustrator of children's stories, Hailey was always interested in learning what thoughts her children had. She sometimes used them for ideas in her books.

Luna could already read and loved to make up stories. "A boy and his two sisters decided to go to the beach. They met another boy who could fly. But he had no home, so the boy and his sisters built this castle for him."

"Very interesting," said Hailey. "I love that the boy and his sisters saw that though he had special powers, there was something important missing in his life, and they did something to help him find a place he could go where he'd always be welcome."

"Of course," Luna said. "Like you in your books."

"I love you," Hailey said, hugging Luna to her. She tucked that little story away to see if it could be worked into one of her Charlie and Zeke stories. Though she'd written other books, her favorites were about the little boy Charlie and his dachshund, Zeke, who were always discovering different life experiences.

The real Zeke ran over to her. Wagging his tail, he

looked up at her with a doggy smile. She leaned over and patted him. Zeke was Nick's first gift to her, and she loved him dearly.

Not to be left out, Tiger joined them, trying to push Zeke aside to get attention for himself.

"Now, Tiger," Hailey said. "There's enough to go around. Wait your turn."

"That's what you say to us," Luna said, picking up Tiger and hugging him.

Hailey smiled. Of the three children, Luna was the one who seemed to need her most. Perhaps by being the middle child or maybe because she had such a loving nature herself.

"Time to go back to the house. Daddy will be here soon, and then it'll be dinnertime," said Hailey.

"Dad said he'd practice the guitar with me," said Brady joining them.

"He promised April and me a tea party," said Luna.

"He'll have time for all of you," said Hailey. "You'll have to take turns."

She and Nick had set up this routine early on, when, with three children under five, Hailey had needed time alone, and by turning the hour or so before dinner over to Nick, she had some freedom to read or do whatever she wanted before preparing their meal. They both agreed, however, to eat dinner together. There were evenings when it wasn't possible or necessarily pleasant, but the children learned pretty quickly what was acceptable behavior. Mostly, it worked.

Still, Hailey and Nick savored their private moments after the kids were in bed. That was their time to discuss the day with a cup of hot coffee, a cold drink, or a glass of wine before tumbling into bed themselves.

Back at the house, when Nick walked through the door he was met by kids and dogs. Hailey never tired of seeing the pleasure on his face as he greeted them with hugs and smiles. He still taught music at the University of South Florida in Tampa and played in a band at some of the clubs in the area. At one time, he'd been a famous rock star worldwide, but now he was more of a local celebrity, which was fine with him. Before they'd met, he'd decided to leave the rock group and get away from the price of real fame.

Hailey waited her turn and then kissed him. "Welcome home. I guess you've promised the girls a tea party and Brady a practice session. I'm going to take a walk along the beach."

Hearing the word 'walk,' Zeke and Tiger trotted over to her.

"Okay," she said. "I guess the dogs are going with me."

He laughed. "Have a nice private time. The kids and I will be fine."

Hailey marveled at how easily Nick had taken on the role of father to these children. He'd always supported his niece, but having children of your own was a different, deeper experience.

She left the house and headed back to the beach. Solitary walks along the water's edge were a healthy way to collect her thoughts and come up with new ideas for her books. She was working on one called *A Home for Henry*, the story of a naughty little rabbit who ran away after being scolded by his mother. As usual, the story would have a happy ending, but there had to be enough angst in the story to keep a child's attention.

Hailey stuck her toe into the lacy foam at the water's edge and then stepped into the Gulf's water until she was ankle-deep. Standing there, lifting her face to the blue sky above her, Hailey let out a sigh of satisfaction. She loved seeing the seagulls and terns spread their wings and glide through the air, crying out for the pleasure of it. Behind her, sandpipers, sanderlings, and other shore birds scurried along the sand, leaving their tiny footprints behind as a reminder of their presence.

Zeke and Tiger, tired from their afternoon running around with the children, walked with her as she made her way down the stretch of the beach to a public entrance where she could sit for a while.

She needed to think. She'd received a call from her agent that morning telling her a toy company wanted the license to use characters in her stories for a series of stuffed toys that would be sold along with special editions of her books—smaller books that young children could hold. Hailey was both excited and worried about such an offer.

She wondered if others understood how carefully drawn, how personal each little character was to her. Would sending those stuffed characters out into the world to be trampled or even forgotten be right? Charlie and Zeke and other characters were her "children" before Brady, Luna, and April came along. But maybe, like real children, her characters needed to be set free to grow.

She stopped. Ahead of her a cattle egret moved on stately long legs wading in the shallow water looking for a meal. Her imagination set a crown upon its head and a royal-blue cloak around its body. Laughing at herself for such foolishness, she continued on her way, carefully bypassing the bird. Even Zeke and Tiger seemed to know not to disturb the creature.

She reached the wooden benches placed in the sand by the public entrance and took a seat. The air was hot and humid, and it felt wonderful to sit for a while. The dogs hovered by the foot showers placed near the walk-way. She ran water for them, then took a sip from the bottle of water she always carried on her walks.

An onshore breeze helped to cool her skin. She sat watching the people around her either lazing in the sun or playing in the water. Farther down, a group of people were playing volleyball. Life on the beach was something she'd never tire of, even though she missed the mountains of home in Idaho.

"Hey, there."

Hailey turned as her friend Janna Garrett approached carrying her toddler son. Zoe, her step-daughter, followed. The same age as Brady, Zoe was a sweet girl who'd helped Brady make the transition to Hailey's home.

"Hi, Auntie Hailey," Zoe said. "Where's Brady? And the girls?"

"They're home. I'm having some 'me' time," Hailey said, winking at her.

Zoe wiggled a toe in the sand and looked up at Janna. "Yeah, Mom sometimes needs time alone too."

"If I sit a moment with Hailey, will you watch Mikey?" Janna asked Zoe. "I won't be long, I promise."

"Okay, but you said we could go see a movie," said Zoe.

"I did," Janna agreed. "Dad will watch Mikey while you and I have special girl time."

Zoe smiled and took Mikey by the hand.

"Stay right where I can see you," warned Janna. She gave Hailey a quick hug. "Missed you at the library the other day. How are things?"

"Fine," Hailey said. "How are you feeling?"

"A bit pregnant," said Janna, "but we're thrilled that we're having a little girl. Zoe most of all."

"It does my heart good to see how things turned out with you and Mike," said Hailey.

"If it hadn't been for you, we might never have met," said Janna smiling. She smoothed her round stomach. "Now look at me."

Hailey returned the smile. Janna still worked, part time now, at the Platt Regional Library where they'd met and where Hailey still did story hours for kids.

They watched as Mikey escaped Zoe's grasp and raced across the sand away from them.

Janna jumped to her feet. "Gotta go. We'll catch up later."

"Yes," said Hailey. "I'd like to talk to you about a plan my agent has."

"Can you get away for a cup of coffee tomorrow morning?" Janna asked.

11

"Yes. I'll make sure I can," said Hailey before Janna turned and jogged away.

Hailey remembered the first year after Brady and Luna came to them. A newborn, Luna required a lot of physical attention while Brady needed help coming to grips with losing his mother and father. Janna's husband, Mike, a clinical psychologist, had helped them through the challenges. Even now, she loved that she could ask him about concerns she had.

Grateful for their friendship, Hailey headed home in a better frame of mind. Janna was a wonderful librarian with a lot of resources and would have some wise tips for her.

Now that the dogs had rested, they trotted along beside her as she walked along the hard-packed sand at the water's edge. This time, the dogs gave no mercy to shore birds who dared to intrude on their path. Zeke, the leader as always, loved charging the birds and seeing them scoot out of his way. Tiger would take care of any who lingered.

When she reached the house, she heard the sound of music. A natural teacher, Nick loved playing with Brady and teaching him new things. Brady was a quick learner and very talented. Because they had little information on Brady's background, Hailey could only suspect that talent came from his mother. In addition to playing the guitar, Brady was taking piano lessons. Not as "cool" for him, but important.

As she walked inside, the girls rushed toward her wearing tiaras. "Did you have a princess party?" she asked, smiling at them.

"Yes, but Daddy is playing music with Brady now," said Luna, making a face.

"Well, would you like to help me fix dinner?" Hailey said.

Luna shook her head. "No, I guess I'll read a book instead."

Hailey hugged her. "That's my girl. You know I loved to read as a little girl." She didn't mention that she'd had to wear thick eyeglasses as a girl, and the pictures in books were mostly what she looked at until her foster mom turned adoptive mother, Maddie Kirby, encouraged her to focus on the words.

"I want to draw, Mommy," said April.

"And so, you shall," said Hailey cheerfully. She went to a kitchen drawer where she kept supplies and took out sheets of paper and a small box of crayons. "You can sit at the table while I cook, and then you can help set the places there." With her 4th birthday coming up in November, April was perfectly capable of doing her share of the work. She remembered how proud she had been as a young girl helping Maddie in the kitchen. It was an excellent way to train children to participate in getting work done.

After making the spaghetti sauce everyone loved, Hailey let it simmer on the stove while she went to find Nick and Brady. Though Nick and his fellow band members rented space in Tampa where they could practice and record music, the "library" in the house had been turned into a music room for Brady and Nick.

She stood outside the door a moment, and listened to Brady's voice soar as he sang a refrain from a popular song. The tone was lovely, so pure that tears stung her eyes. He was such a sweet boy that it seemed only natural for him to have a singing voice like this.

When the music ended, she tapped on the door.

Nick came to it. "Dinner ready?"

"Just about. Time for everyone to wash their hands and come to the table."

Nick put his arm around her and drew her close. "Can't wait until later. I have some news to share."

"Me, too," she said. It was sometimes irritating to have to put off their quiet time together, but she and Nick had discovered it was the easiest way with three active children wanting their attention.

Nick gave her a kiss that filled her with anticipation, and then she headed for the kitchen, thinking she'd never loved him more. She adored their family—a tight little unit—and hoped nothing would destroy it.

CHAPTER 2

After the children were settled in bed, Nick and Hailey sat on the lanai enjoying the cooler night air.

"How about a glass of wine?" Nick said. "Coffee will keep me awake tonight."

Curious, she said, "What's going on?"

"Hold on," said Nick. "I'll be right back with the wine. I want to celebrate."

Hailey sat, looking out at the water, hearing the waves kiss the shore and pull back again in a rhythm as old as time. She loved the sound of it, the smell of the salty air.

Nick returned and handed her a glass of wine. "Here's to us and our children."

Puzzled, Hailey clicked her glass against his. "Okay, now you have to tell me. No secrets."

"I didn't realize when Brady and I tried out for the local talent show that a producer was watching. Jonnie

Dobbs is well respected in the music world with releases under his own label – Horizon Records. He wants to do a record of well-known children's songs with me on guitar and Brady singing."

"Just the two of you?" asked Hailey.

"Well, with background accompaniment, but featuring us," said Nick. "Isn't that great?"

Hailey paused. When she and Nick first met, he was a well-known musician and had turned away from it. Now he wanted to this. *What would it do to him? And Brady? And the rest of them?* Her mind spun.

"I think it's a wonderful validation of the music you share with Brady. But I don't want him to be in the public eye. He doesn't need that kind of attention."

"I agree," said Nick, "which is why I like this idea. There will be no need to perform in public. It's just a recording for young children that won't require live performances. I think he'd like to do it, especially if he's considering music as a career."

"Let's talk to Brady about it and see how he feels. I'd also like to get Mike's opinion on it," said Hailey.

"Fair enough. For me, it's simply a fun project, something for kids." He smiled at her. "What's your news?"

Hailey told him about the call from her agent and the toy company that wanted to get a license to use her characters.

He beamed at her. "Sounds great? What's the problem?"

"I guess the problem is me. Those characters are like members of my fantasy family. I'm not sure how I feel about doing this."

Nick took hold of her hand. "Aw, Hailey, you're such a mom. Have you thought of those characters helping kids? Tying them into your stories so they have something to hold onto?"

Hailey nodded. "Yes, which is why I'm willing to consider the idea. I know it's a wise move financially, but I want to be able to have some input into how they're treated."

"We'll get the best intellectual property lawyer we can find," Nick said. "We'll take care of your fantasy characters." He got up from his seat, walked over to the couch where she was sitting, and drew her up into his arms. "I'm proud of you, Hailey, for your work and how much you care about it."

She smiled. "And I'm proud of the music you're making with Brady." She chuckled softly. "Looks like our family is growing in ways we would've never predicted."

"It'll all be good," said Nick.

"I hope so," said Hailey. Life had already handed them a lot of surprises.

The next morning, she eagerly joined Janna at Beans, a local coffee shop, for a long over-due chat with her best friend.

She and Janna had connected from their first meeting when Hailey had approached a local library for doing a story hour from time to time. Having been a librarian in charge of the children's section in her hometown, Hailey wanted to continue to read to kids.

JUDITH KEIM

While Janna couldn't replace her sisters, they were very close.

Janna slid into the booth opposite Hailey and smiled. "What's up? You wanted to talk."

Hailey told her about the deal the toy company was interested in and then said, "Do you think it's a good idea? I worry about losing control of the characters."

Janna took a sip of coffee and set her cup down. "I know how important they are to you, but sometimes you have to take a leap forward and trust that things will go well. Besides, you will, no doubt, have excellent legal counsel."

"You're right. I needed to hear that from you. Nick thinks I should do it too."

"Then, do it," said Janna, squeezing her hand.

Though she trusted Nick, Hailey liked that Janna was as straightforward with her. "Guess we'd better get back to the library. "

"I'm liking this part-time job more and more as a much-needed break," said Janna.

Hailey laughed, remembering her pregnancy with April and how a trip to the library turned into an escape.

After talking over her fears with both Janna and also Mike, Hailey decided to look into the offer with the toy company and also agreed with Nick to approach Brady about the record deal.

That afternoon, she and Nick sat with Brady in the music room.

Nick explained about the record deal, that it would be a one-time thing with no stage appearances, and that it would be for children.

Brady listened and then slowly nodded. "I get to play the guitar with you, Dad?"

Nick nodded.

"Okay, then, I want to do it. I remember someone singing to me. My mother, I think."

"I'm sure she'd be thrilled to know you have such a lovely voice," said Hailey. "I can write and draw, but I can't sing at all."

Brady grinned. "But you're my mom and a good cook."

Hailey hugged him to her. He was such a special boy. Always had been. She remembered when she first met him, he was quiet, hardly speaking. An instant connection to him had been created because of her own unwillingness to speak openly as a young child.

"Okay, then, we've agreed we'll go ahead with it," said Nick. "We'll have to take care of all the legal matters and then we can do it. Thank you, son, for being honest with us. I'm proud of the way you can sing, and I'm happy to share it with others."

"Can I go out now? Zoe is meeting me on the beach," said Brady.

Hailey and Nick exchanged amused smiles. Those two kids were always thinking of something to do together. Maybe time would change that, but for now, it was cute.

After he left, Nick said, "It'll be pretty simple to come up with a contract for Brady and me. How are you doing with your agent?"

"She's doing some investigation on her own. But I've told her we'll have our own lawyer take a look at any contract too. And she's fine with that."

"Good. Now let's take some time to ourselves. Do you want to go out to dinner tonight? We might still be able to get into Gavin's at the Salty Key Inn."

"The idea of a delicious meal and a little pampering sound fantastic. Taylor should be available." Nick had come up with the idea of paying Taylor Ryder a monthly fee to insure she'd be available whenever they called. They were careful not to abuse her time, but as a struggling college student Taylor loved the idea. When she wasn't needed for babysitting, she cheerfully helped Hailey with administrative work. After following this arrangement for four years, Taylor was more like a big sister than a babysitter.

That evening, Hailey stood in front of her closet trying to decide what to wear. Growing up, her sisters had often helped her with her wardrobe. Now she depended on Janna for input. Though there was nothing wrong with her body, she was short and on the thin side and required clothes that were more classic than cute.

She pulled out a gray-linen sleeveless sheath. That, with some new turquoise jewelry would do. Luna and April lounged on the king-size bed watching her every move as they'd done when she'd put on makeup. Delighted when she put a tiny bit of lipstick on their lips, the girls studied the necklace Hailey held up for them to view.

"That's good, Mommy," said Luna, giving her a nod of approval.

April climbed off of the bed, hurried over to the closet, and pulled out a pair of shiny pink flip-flops. "Wear these, Mommy."

Hailey smiled. "Maybe another time. Thank you."

"No, April," said Luna joining them. "Mommy has to wear these." She held up a pair of strappy black sandals.

"Okay," said Hailey, knowing how important it was to Luna to accept her choice. She'd fuss over April's choice at the appropriate time.

When at last it was time to leave the room to join Nick on the lanai, the girls followed her like eager puppies.

Nick looked up from where he was reading a book and whistled. "My gorgeous wife."

"Mommy is bootiful," said April, clapping her hands and smiling at her.

"See my lipstick," Luna said, climbing into Nick's lap for attention.

"Bootiful," he said, winking at Hailey. He hugged Luna and got to his feet. "We'd better go. The hostess at Gavin's did me a favor and squeezed us in. I don't want to be late."

Saying farewell was a production Hailey never tired of. She kissed each of the children, patted the dogs on their heads, and said goodbye to Taylor, feeling as if she and Nick were dating. She glanced at him as he helped her into his car, thinking back to the rock star he'd been and the wonderful family man he'd become.

Sitting inside Gavin's restaurant, Hailey relaxed. Though they weren't the kind of couple that needed to go out constantly to have fun, being here with Nick away from the demands of the children was as delicious as the food she knew she'd enjoy.

She took a moment to look around at the dark wood on the walls, the crystal wall sconces and the little garden outside the window beside her. Soft light from the crystal chandeliers cast a warm glow, enhancing the setting.

She noticed Petey, the famous peacock that lived on the property and smiled. A year ago, she'd spent time taking photographs of the bird, making note of distinctive qualities about him so she could include him in a new picture book about Charlie and Zeke discovering birds in the area. She'd even created a short poem about him:

> Petey, the peacock, so proud and tall,
> You and your train might be prettiest of all.
> But let's not forget you are but one
> Of other lovely birds unique or small.

"What are you smiling at?" Nick asked her.

"I'm thinking of Petey, the peacock, and how I worked him into a Charlie and Zeke book."

"You're so clever," Nick said. "Have I told you lately how much I love you?"

"No, but you can show me after we get home," she said with a teasing smile. Though they still shared romance it wasn't like the early days when they couldn't keep their hands off one another. Not when they could be interrupted at any moment.

After Nick conferred with the wine steward, they sipped on a pinot grigio as they perused the menu.

Hailey ordered sea bass with a lemon *beurre blanc* while Nick opted for the prime strip steak.

At one point, one of the three sisters who owned the restaurant approached and asked how they were, and if they needed anything.

Nick assured her they were fine, and the stunning redhead moved on to the next table.

Hailey loved the story of the three sisters taking a run-down motel and turning it into the prized property it was today. But then she loved stories of sisters anyway because her own soul sisters meant the world to her. Though they lived in Idaho, they all kept in contact. Hailey, as the youngest at eight when she was brought into the home, would always be grateful to them. Alissa and she had shared a room and from the beginning, had formed a special friendship that continued.

Alissa had started making jams and set up a business before she found she was pregnant with twins. She was a smart, capable woman who'd learned to balance business and babies. Hailey was very proud of her and all her sisters.

Nick reached across the table and squeezed her hand.

She smiled and focused her attention back to him. Heaven knew when they'd have a night out like this again. Often, a night out meant they just grabbed a burger at the Pink Pelican.

After they'd eaten the last bite of a shared *crème brulée*, Hailey was ready to go home with her hunky husband.

After saying goodnight to Taylor, Hailey and Nick went to check on the kids. They peeked inside Brady's room and saw that he was sprawled across the bed as if he'd just thrown himself there after a long run. Tiger lay at his feet.

Hailey blew a kiss to him, afraid to wake him. Of all the kids he was the lightest sleeper. Next, they went to the girls' room. Luna had wanted to share a room with April, something that would no doubt change in the future. For the moment, it was a shared fairyland— every little girl's dream with pink walls and white four-poster beds.

In one bed, Luna lay on her back surrounded by the stuffed animals she loved. In the other, April lay on her side with Zeke cuddled against her back.

Staring at the girls, tears stung Hailey's eyes. She and Nick were very lucky to have such wonderful children.

Nick put a hand on her shoulder and squeezed it, and she knew he was feeling the same way. There was a time when they'd wondered if they'd ever have children of their own.

Hailey followed Nick to their room, thinking it was a perfect night for a dip in the pool. The air was still pleasantly warm, the moon cast a soft glow, and they would have all the privacy they wanted behind the wall that enclosed the back of their lot—an area that included the screened pool and her art studio.

Before she could mention it, Nick turned to her with a grin. "A nice night for a swim."

She laughed. "Great minds think alike. Beat you to the pool!"

Giggling softly, they quickly changed, grabbed towels, and headed outside.

The pool was surrounded by a special safety gate to protect the kids, even though all three knew how to swim. Hailey opened it and went inside. Not having bothered to turn on the pool lights, she slid into the dark water and let out a sigh of appreciation. The moon above gave enough light that she could see clearly as she began to swim. After doing a few laps, Hailey sat on the steps in the shallow end of the pool to cool off.

Nick sat beside her. "You're beautiful, Hailey. It's hard to believe you're a mother of a nine-year-old. Before we know it, the kids will be gone."

"Whoa! Let's not think about that yet. Let's simply enjoy every day with them," Hailey said, chuckling. "I'm just getting used to handling them."

He laughed. "Are you really okay with Brady and me doing that record?"

"Yes," she said. "I think it'll be an enjoyable experience for him.'

"We'll announce it at the talent show." Nick smiled. "I'm pretty sure we're going to win."

"A little overconfident, are we?" she teased.

"Just wanting to keep good energy about it," he said laughing. "Let's go inside. I have more good energy to show you."

Hailey smiled and took his hand. She could hardly wait.

CHAPTER 3

Hailey sat in the audience with her girls. Janna, Mike, and Zoe sat next to her in the same row of seats. Her insides were a tingle of nerves. She'd been so shy as a child she hardly spoke. To think Brady had no problem singing in front of an audience amazed her. She thought of his mother, and sent a whisper of a thought into the air. *Linnie, you would be very proud of him.*

It was interesting to see what talents other people brought to the show that benefitted the local high school baseball program. But as Nick and Brady began to perform one of Nick's new original songs, it was clear who the winners would be. Hearing the two of them sing together, with Nick harmonizing to Brady's clear soprano voice, Hailey thought it was magical. As they finished singing, she applauded with the rest of the audience, blinded by tears.

The winners were announced, confirming Nick and Brady were by far the best. As he accepted the award,

Nick took the opportunity to tell the audience about the record he and Brady were working on. "Just a heads up," he said. "We'll be letting you know more about it in the future." He put his arm around Brady. "I'm really proud of my son. Brady, take a bow."

Grinning, Brady bobbed his head and then shuffled his feet.

Moments later, Hailey was talking with Janna when Brady ran over to her.

"Look, Mom! Dad and I won!" He held up a blue ribbon.

"I see," she said, giving him a hug. "Congratulations."

He smiled. "I wasn't scared."

"I think we have a natural performer," said Nick, joining them.

"I saw you, Daddy," said April, taking hold of his hand.

Nick picked her up. "I noticed you sitting with Mommy."

"Did you see me?" asked Luna.

Nick laughed and ruffled her hair. "I always see you, Luna." He set April down on her feet and turned to Mike. "What did you think?"

"You have a real star on your hands," Mike answered. "He seems to like it."

At Mike's response, Hailey tensed. She was fine with Brady performing in a talent show and singing on a record, but she wasn't sure she wanted a "young star" in the household. That sounded almost dangerous.

All the way home, Hailey thought about Mike's words. She was happy Brady enjoyed music, but she didn't want the life of a music star for him or for the rest of them.

It wasn't until after the kids were in bed that night that Hailey had the opportunity to voice her concern to Nick.

"I don't want our lives to be focused around one person," Hailey explained, turning to face him in bed.

Nick nodded thoughtfully. "I understand. Let's take it one step at a time and give Brady a chance to explore music while not pushing him for something beyond enjoyment."

"Okay, thanks," said Hailey. "I don't know why I feel strongly about this, but the idea of including everyone in our family is important to me."

"Considering your background, it's understand-able." Nick drew her against him and rubbed her back. "You make ours special."

"I learned from the best," Hailey said. "Maddie was the most wonderful mother to my sisters and me."

"And now you're doing the same for our kids," said Nick, pressing his lips against hers.

As Nick continued to hold her close, talk of the children turned to something else.

For the next several days, Hailey remained busy with her normal routines and trying to finish her latest book. She'd also begun the process of going through legal matters with the toy company.

One afternoon, when she went to pick up the girls at preschool, April's teacher pulled Hailey aside. "I believe April may have a problem seeing. You might want to get her eyes checked."

Hailey's heart fell. She'd had to wear thick glasses as a young child. She hoped April wouldn't have to do the same. Being teased for it had been traumatic for Hailey, but then she'd learned early on not to draw attention to herself, or she'd be punished by cruel foster parents.

Hailey set up an eye appointment right away. When the optometrist declared that April had myopia, Hailey wasn't surprised. She'd suffered from nearsightedness herself as a child. As they went about looking at frames, Hailey worked hard to keep up her enthusiasm, helping to choose glasses that would be attractive. They settled on a pair of light-blue frames that brought out the blue in April's eyes and ordered lenses that turned dark in the sun so April would be protected outdoors.

"Do I have to wear them, Mommy?" April asked, with a definite whine.

"Yes, but you'll get used to them. I promise," Hailey said, her words catching in her throat as she hugged her. "You look adorable in them because your blue eyes are very pretty."

When she had a moment of privacy, she called her mom and told her about April's need for glasses. "I feel sorry for her," Hailey ended.

"Sweetie, you were cute with or without glasses. The important thing is for April to see without straining her eyes. In time, she'll be able to wear contacts and have corrective surgery."

"You're right, Mom. Besides, April has a lot more confidence than I ever did at her age."

"True, but look at you now," said her mother,

sending a surge of love through Hailey. Her mother had always made her see herself at her best.

They chatted about her sisters and other things, and when Hailey hung up, she felt much better.

But Hailey was still sensitive about the issue as she reviewed the paperwork for the toy company and noticed they'd decided to draw their Charlie figure without glasses.

Hailey called her agent right away. Rachel Robbins was a smart woman who usually supported Hailey's ideas. "Good afternoon, Rachel," said Hailey, holding in her temper. "Can you explain why the toy company is planning to design Charlie without glasses?"

"As a matter of fact, I asked that question myself. Their answer is they're afraid the glasses will get lost or broken and they'll get complaints. Better to do without them, they said."

"In that case, I'm withdrawing from the project. The contract is off," Hailey said crisply.

"Whoa, wait a minute. What's going on, Hailey?" Rachel asked in a soothing voice.

Hailey drew a deep breath, fighting off memories. "As a kid who had to wear glasses and the mother of a child who needs them, I think those glasses are very important. You can't imagine the letters I've received from parents thanking me for drawing a character with glasses."

"So, it's a personal issue. I see. Let me talk to someone there and get back to you. Are you all right?"

"Just feeling a little stressed," said Hailey. "I'm sorry, but it's a sensitive subject for me. Please let me know how you do with the toy company. Hope all is well in your world."

"Yes, busy as usual, but that's the biz," said Rachel. "Don't worry. We'll get the matter resolved."

"Thanks," said Hailey, ending the call. She sat in her office and looked out at the waves, telling herself to calm down, but her first instinct always was to protect her children, even though she knew life would hand them a few blows.

Later, when Nick arrived home, he held up the local weekly newspaper. "There's a story about Brady and me in the talent show. A human-interest kind of thing."

Hailey read the article about Nick and Brady. It told how they had adopted Brady and were now a close-knit group, with father and son making music together.

"Nice, huh?" said Nick.

"It's sweet," agreed Hailey. "Something to put in Brady's scrap book." Hailey had set up a scrap book for each of the children. In Brady and Luna's case, she'd wanted what photos she could find of Linnie and Mac to be included. Otherwise, paintings, photos, and other memorabilia were included.

The kids weren't at all excited about the newspaper story. Even Brady barely looked at it. Hailey breathed a sigh of relief. Maybe she didn't have to worry about him needing to be the center of attention. Especially now that football season was in full swing, and he and Nick spent time watching their favorite team, the Bucs.

Life continued to be full. Luna was taking classes in gymnastics, and April started a toddler ballet program she loved.

Hailey was pleased. Everyone was happy and busy,

the toy company added glasses for Charlie, and Hailey's new book was starting to come together.

She was alone in the house when the dogs started barking and milling around the front door. She went to them and checked through the opening to see who might be there.

A pretty, blonde-haired woman of average height, wearing a turquoise linen dress and high heels stood facing her. Hailey guessed she was in her mid-fifties, a few years younger than her mother.

Hailey cracked open the door. "Yes? What can I do for you?"

"I'm sorry to intrude. My name is Missy Macklin. Please hear me out. I have a story to tell you, a personal one. You see," She drew in a deep breath and slowly released it. "I think I may be Brady's grandmother."

Shock froze Hailey. When she finally collected herself, she said very quietly, "I don't think that's possible. I don't know how you found us or why you're saying this. You must understand I'll do anything to protect my child. Any further talk will have to be directed through our lawyer."

"Oh, but I can't go to a lawyer. No one knows about this. Not even my husband." The woman wrung her hands. "It's all been such a surprise to me too. If I hadn't seen the picture of Brady in the recent newspaper article and read the story about your family, I might never have known. Brady is the exact image of his grandfather, Henry Neeley, at that age. I knew and loved Henry when I was growing up. The son I was forced to give up as a teen was named Henry too."

Heart pounding, Hailey held up her hand to stop

her. "As I said, I'm not about to let anybody disrupt my family with stories like this one. This will have to be handled by our attorney. Now, please go."

"I'm sorry if I upset you," the woman said, giving her an apologetic look as she offered Hailey a card. "Here are my name and phone number. Please give me a call. If someone else answers the phone, just say you're calling from the library. I know about you too."

A shiver crossed Hailey's shoulders, but she took the card the woman handed her. As Hailey watched, the woman crossed the front walk and got into a late-model gray sedan.

Hailey memorized the Florida license plate number as the woman drove away, and then she hurried inside to write it down on a pad of paper. She sank into a chair at the kitchen table, too weak to stand. Both of Brady's parents had been in the foster care system like her, which was one reason Hailey had chosen to help Linnie. Someone couldn't just claim to be a grandparent, could they? Especially when there wasn't any way to be sure except through a DNA test, and there was no way Hailey wanted Brady to know anything about this.

She lifted her cell and called Nick.

After she finished telling him about the visit, she blurted, "I was uneasy about publicity for Brady. Now, I know why."

"Hailey, I'm sorry this happened. We'll just have to deal with the situation. Before we call a lawyer, we need to see what information we can find out about this woman. You say you got the automobile license number? That'll help. But there's got to be a lot more information we can find online. Gotta go. My class is ready. We'll talk tonight."

Hailey ended the call and let out a shaky sigh. Neither one had mentioned it, but Hailey wondered if there would be a request for money along the way. She was well-known for her books and was financially successful, and Nick was known for his music.

As soon as she'd gathered more information about Missy Macklin, she'd call Owen Sheehan, the family law attorney they'd used when they'd adopted Brady and Luna,

Hailey went into her office and sat in front of the computer with a notepad and pen. She took a deep breath and typed in 'Missy Macklin Florida.' No relevant listing came up. Next, she tried just 'Macklin in Florida.' Again, no relevant listing came up.

Stumped, she tried to think. The best information she had was the license plate number. She called Janna. Through her work at the library and meeting a lot of people, Janna might know of someone who might be helpful.

Janna answered the phone sleepily. "Hi, Hailey. What's up?"

"I need your help," Hailey said trying desperately to prevent her voice from quivering.

"What's going on?" Janna asked, sounding wide awake now.

Hailey explained the situation. "The best information I have for Missy Macklin is the license plate number. Do you know of anyone who could get the name of the person who owns that for me?"

"Maybe," Janna said. "But don't ask me who or how.

Give me the number and I'll get back to you as soon as I can." Her take-charge attitude soothed Hailey.

After giving Janna the information, Hailey ended the call, left her studio, and went back inside the house. As if a spider's web had caught hold of her, Hailey was drawn to Brady's room, the center of her worry.

Standing at the doorway, Hailey looked around. At nine, Brady was interested in many things. An old publicity poster from Nick's band days hung on the wall along with a picture of the Tampa Bay Buccaneers, and a meme from one of his computer games.

She walked into the room and sat on his bed, needing to feel close to him. As she'd told Missy Macklin, she'd do anything to protect her child. Still, the woman who'd approached her was well-spoken, well-dressed, and obviously distraught. What if she was telling the truth?

Janna called. "The license plate is issued to a car rental agency in Miami."

"Is that it?" Hailey asked.

"Don't ask me any questions. That's all I can tell you. I don't like to take advantage of the connections I have," said Janna. "Wish I could be of more help. You know I'd do anything for you."

"Yes, I do. Thanks. How are you feeling?" Hailey asked, hiding her disappointment.

"Most days, I'm fine. Today, is one of those days when Mikey can't settle down and is into everything. I'm exhausted. I don't know how you did it when you were pregnant with April."

"I don't know either," said Hailey, remembering

those hectic times. "Thanks again. Feel better soon." She ended the call and phoned Owen's office.

The receptionist explained that he was out of the office, but she would have him phone her. Feeling helpless, Hailey clicked off the call and stared into space.

When it was time to pick up the girls from preschool, Hailey pushed aside her worries and placed a smile on her face as she greeted them.

Observing Luna and April walking toward her together, a thought struck her. Missy Macklin hadn't mentioned Luna. Would that keep Luna safe for the time being?

CHAPTER 4

Hailey waited at the school bus stop for Brady. Ordinarily he and Jason Pierce, another boy in the neighborhood, walked the short distance home together. Today, Hailey wasn't comfortable giving him that freedom. Missy hadn't seemed the kind of woman who'd resort to something violent, but who knew if she was working for someone else. Hailey was aware those thoughts seemed melodramatic, but she had to be sure he was safe.

"Hi, Mom," Brady shouted, waving as he hopped off the bus.

Hailey's heart clenched at the thought of anyone taking Brady from her.

"Hi, buddy," she said, attempting to sound as casual as possible. "I thought I'd surprise you. Hi, Jason. Let's walk home together."

Jason nodded but couldn't hide the frown on his brow.

"I know you're both growing up, but sometimes it's

nice for me to walk with you," Hailey said. She and Jason's mother had made a big deal about the boys walking together for safety while acknowledging their independence.

The boys went ahead of her and finally sprinted into their cove neighborhood. Hailey studied the area around her, looking for the gray sedan Missy had been driving and was satisfied when there was no sign of it. Still, worry gnawed at her.

When Nick walked through the door that evening, he looked around. "Where are the kids?"

"I gave them permission to watch some television," Hailey said. "I wanted the chance to give you an update on Missy Macklin."

"Okay, let's go to your studio where we can talk privately." He kissed her. "I know you've been worrying about this, but we'll work things out, keep our kids safe." He put an arm around her shoulder, and they walked outside.

As happened every time she entered her studio, a sense of pride filled her. The small adobe building with a skylight and plenty of windows was the perfect space for her work. A large section of one wall was covered in cork for use as a bulletin board where she could hang some of the drawings she was working on. She did drawings in pencil before doing watercolors to be sure to get details right. Gazing at the familiar characters, she smiled. They were, as she'd described to Nick earlier, almost real to her.

They headed to the couch that she had placed along one wall of the studio, and sat down.

Hailey gave Nick as many details as she could. "Owen will call tomorrow. I told the receptionist it was urgent. And Nick, I think it's time for another talk with the kids about strangers. I don't want to frighten them, but it's important."

"I agree," Nick said. "Why don't we do it at the dinner table where we have everyone's attention."

"The whole idea of a grandparent wanting to see a grandchild after not being part of her child's life is both spooky and admirable," said Hailey. "Every kid in foster care wants someone truly to care about them because they feel abandoned already. I was lucky that Maddie took me in when she did. How awful to think of Mac wondering about his mother, not knowing how much she'd wanted him."

"I understand, but this could be a tragic mistake if it's not handled properly. Let's talk to Owen and have him get in touch with Missy Macklin. If she should appear again, tell her you're going to call the cops if she doesn't leave." Nick studied her. "Agreed?"

Hailey nodded. "I don't want anything to happen to Brady, or any of the kids." The tears that had threatened all day slid down her cheeks.

Nick wrapped his arm around her and stroked her back in comforting circles. "We'll make sure it doesn't. If you want, Brady and I won't perform together anymore."

Hailey stared into the distance seeing the joy on Brady's face as he sang with his father. "No, Nick. Let's not do that. Let him enjoy singing with you right here at home. We can make a better decision later."

"We've been asked to participate in the Christmas musical the Chamber of Commerce puts on every year. But I'll tell them I won't be able to confirm until later."

"Thanks. Let's go in. I need to get dinner ready." Their relaxing dinner at Gavin's seemed eons ago.

The next morning when Owen called, Hailey was ready with a list of questions. After filling in the details for him, Hailey said, "Nick and I would like you to call her and follow up with any information. As I told you, I found nothing online about Missy. She mentioned the boyfriend with whom she had the baby was a man named Henry Neeley. She also told me that no one else has any knowledge of it."

"Let me put one of my interns on this," said Owen. "In the meantime, I concur that being overly cautious with Brady's whereabouts is wise. Many strange cases like this can escalate, and we want to be very sure this isn't one of them."

Rather than making her more nervous, Hailey found comfort in his words. They would work together to protect Brady.

Trying to keep her worries at bay, Hailey dove into her work on the book about Henry the unlucky rabbit who was about to learn a lesson. It seemed a little odd to be writing about the sweet little creature when Missy's story of her boyfriend, Henry, and the little boy they had together circled in her head.

Two days later, Hailey received a phone call from Owen's office asking her to come in and meet with him. Her nerves tingling with the possibilities of the information her lawyer had uncovered, she dressed and drove into St. Petersburg to meet with him.

His office was in an attractive four-story building in the downtown area. Hailey parked and got out of the car tense from not knowing what awaited her. The fact that Owen wanted to meet in person wasn't an encouraging sign. Or was it? She was so nervous.

Warning herself not to panic with each step she took, she went into the office and informed the receptionist who she was.

Owen soon appeared. "Hi, Hailey. Nice to see you. Come on back to my office to discuss the news I have for you."

He led her back to an unremarkable room with a nice view of palm trees outside.

Have a seat," he said, indicating one of the chairs in front of his desk.

Her legs collapsed as she sank into the brown-leather chair. "What is it? Good news?"

From behind his desk, Owen studied her. "Interesting news." He drew a breath and let it out slowly. "The reason you couldn't find anything on Missy Macklin is because that is her maiden name. Her married name is Missy Linley. The phone number she gave you is real though. When I called, a woman answered with the words 'the Linley residence." When I asked if Missy was there, Missy quickly got on the call.

I told her I was representing you and Nick, and that I was aware that she'd made an unannounced visit to you. A visit that was clearly upsetting. I told her that any communication going forward would have to be through me."

"How did she react to that?" Hailey asked.

"She was quiet and then she agreed to that request," said Owen. "I gave her my email address so she can send me what information she wants us to have. She also agreed to a DNA test, should we request it. I told her we needed specific information from her to enable us to decide how to go forward." Owen studied Hailey. "She gave no signs of lying or being insincere. However, she cautioned that her husband is a very successful businessman, and neither he nor any friends have knowledge of her previous teenage trouble."

"Does she have other children?" Hailey asked.

"I asked that," said Owen, "and she told me she was unable to conceive during their marriage."

"What a tragedy to have a child taken away without the ability to have more," said Hailey.

"If that's true," cautioned Owen. "We're still checking details. I suggest we hire a detective to find out what we can about Missy Linley beyond what we've been able to discover online. I suggest you do your own research, just to satisfy yourself that this person exists. You mentioned she was a pleasant-looking women. Her pictures online agree with that."

"What is her husband like? I wonder why she couldn't tell him about this," said Hailey.

"He was a formidable businessman, an owner of more than one property in the city. Now, I understand he suffers from Alzheimer's, which is why she might be free to investigate. All of this will come out in future communication with her. I asked her to put together a summary of facts that would convince us to want to follow through on this issue. Otherwise, we'll initiate a cease-and-desist order with the court."

"So, it's up to her to convince me to speak with her? Is that what you're telling me?" said Hailey.

Owen bobbed his head. "Essentially. In the meantime, I'll give you a list of names and events to research on your own, so you're comfortable if you should want to go forward."

"Do you think there's any danger to Brady?" Hailey asked. "If Missy's wealthy, could she hire someone to take Brady away? I know that sounds far-fetched, but stranger things have happened."

"I don't believe Missy is that kind of person. And from the way she talked, I don't think she wants her husband or their friends to know about her background. Apparently, it's a rags-to riches story."

"That makes sense to me. If you get any communication from her, I'd appreciate having the ability to read it."

"Absolutely. Let's see what, if anything, she does to communicate, and I'll be in touch with you. This is one of those situations that's filled with both caution and hope. With a lot of adoptees trying to find birth parents and vice versa, not all, but a lot of happy endings have occurred."

"Let's hope this is one of them," said Hailey, not at all sure how she wanted this to play out. She loved her situation as it was and didn't know if she wanted some woman claiming to be Brady's grandmother to be part of it. That's why Missy would have to prove to her that it was best for everyone for her to be involved. And if this was some kind of sick joke, she wanted Brady never to know about it.

She left Owen's office with a list of names to look up online. As she drove home, she thought of Missy wanting to hide her background. Coming from a poor, unstable beginning until Maddie took her in to give her a loving home, Hailey understood that.

In her office, Hailey spent time looking up information on Missy Linley. In New York City, Missy was a socialite. Picture after picture showed her at one event after another, beautiful but not smiling.

In those same photos, her husband exuded power. He had broad shoulders and a short, powerful body and usually wore a stern look on his sharp-featured face. Hailey got the impression Wallace Linley was not an easy man to please and was surprised by how deeply she felt sorry for Missy. She wondered how Alzheimer's disease was affecting him.

The company Wallace owned—a real estate holding company—had recently been sold for multiple millions of dollars. As a result, Wallace was being sued by his ex-partner for breaking an agreement to share profits equally.

Still, she was curious how Missy had managed all these years, and if she was Mac's mother, how she'd handled the loss of her baby. And what happened that caused Mac to end up in foster care? Again, a stream of sympathy washed through her.

Hailey did a search on Missy's hometown, a small town in Pennsylvania near the New York State border. She could imagine how difficult it was for Missy to be pregnant in her teens. There was mention of a man named Neeley who owned a drug store but no specific name of Henry Neeley.

Hailey stood and gazed out at the palm trees. In the onshore breeze, their fronds rustled, sending whispers in the air as if they, too, had secrets to share. She thought of the woman who'd come to her door claiming Brady was a part of her. She hadn't seemed crazy, but maybe she was.

Sighing heavily, Hailey headed back to the house. Her first concern had to be for Nick and her children. Now it was time to pick up the girls, and then Brady would come home.

CHAPTER 5

Hailey couldn't stop thinking of Missy. The thought of a baby being given to people who then couldn't take care of him haunted her dreams. As often as she could in her busy schedule, she began research on Mac.

And when Owen told her he had more information for her, Hailey eagerly read through it.

Going through the notes Missy had sent was almost like sneaking a peek inside someone's diary. Hailey learned that Missy's family was poor in a poor town. Her father drank and couldn't hold a job. Her mother worked as a cleaning woman and was sometimes paid in food so she and her daughter could eat. Because she was very bright, her teachers urged Missy to study hard with college in mind. Henry Neeley's parents owned the local drugstore in town, and her seventh-grade English teacher helped Missy get a part-time job there. She and Henry quickly fell in love. Because of their different backgrounds, they had to keep their feelings private. Henry was destined to go on to better things.

Hailey set down her coffee mug and sighed. What she'd read indicated a failed romance from the start. She went back to her screen to read more.

When Missy discovered she was pregnant, she had no one to turn to. She broke it off with Henry, left town, and went to Westchester, Pennsylvania, where an aunt lived. Knowing her mother couldn't handle another mouth to feed, her aunt arranged for Missy to get medical help at a home for unwed mothers. There was no question about her keeping the baby—she was young and poor. Convinced she'd help a couple who desperately wanted a baby, Missy signed adoption papers. But when her baby was born, she changed her mind. And even though she told a nurse she wanted to keep him, the last thing Missy remembered after making that announcement was waking up with the baby having been taken away.

Hailey got to her feet and paced the floor. Why had she herself been left in foster care as an infant? Was her own mother reluctant to give her up? Was her name Hailey Bennett real or had someone changed it along the way as she was bounced from foster home to foster home. The thought of being an unwanted nobody tore at her insides. Maddie Kirby had helped to change those feelings, but at times like this, they came roaring back.

Reminded to make sure Brady and Luna knew they'd been loved by their parents and were now loved by Nick and her, Hailey decided to step outside for a breath of fresh air. Normally she loved the smell of her studio filled with the odor of paints, charcoal pencils, and other art supplies. Filled with painful memories, she now found it stifling.

She crossed the lawn, opened the gate, and walked out onto the sand, the dogs behind her. She thought of the sandcastles she and the children built and decided to place Missy mentally inside the next one they built. Missy may or may not be related to Brady, but she deserved love anyway. For now, Missy would remain unknown to the children.

Hailey walked to the water's edge and wiggled her toes in the lacy froth the waves left behind. The water still held summer's warmth but would grow colder in the days ahead. She lifted her face to the sun and took a deep breath of the salty air to calm her thoughts. She thought of Linnie and Mac. They'd both been in foster care and had found happiness with one another. It was a testament to the idea that we all needed love. She hadn't known Mac, but she'd seen the strength in Linnie, a true survivor.

Impatient with the disturbing thoughts in her mind, Hailey took off running. Barking, Zeke and Tiger followed her. Though Tiger was able to run faster, out of love for Zeke he circled ahead of her to rejoin Zeke at her feet.

Hailey slowed her steps and caught her breath. Seeing the waves roll in and pull away, she took comfort in the steady movement. Somehow, the mess with Missy would get sorted out.

That night after the children were in bed, she sat on the lanai with Nick.

Sitting beside her on the couch, he turned to her. "What is it, Hailey? You've been quiet today. I know something is troubling you. Is it Missy?"

She nodded. "It's her story, and mine, and also the idea that after struggling to find a place in the world, Linnie and Mac found love with one another." She reached over and cupped his cheek. "I'm very happy to have you, Nick."

"Come here," he whispered hoarsely. He drew her onto his lap and wrapped his arms around her. "I love you, Hailey, and I always will. And I'll always be here for our children. I love them too."

She smiled at him. "I know you do. It's like a miracle when two people find the right person for them in each other. It was such a lucky day when I saw you again at Cedar Mountain Lodge."

"My lucky day, too," said Nick. His lips met hers, and she melted in his arms.

After they pulled away, Nick studied her. "Any new thoughts on what you want to do about Missy?"

"We're still waiting for information from the detective we hired. He'll verify Missy's story, or prove to us that she's lying, or she's simply a woman who desperately wants to make a connection to her lost baby."

"What do *you* think, Hailey?"

"I think she's never forgotten the baby who taken away, but I have to be certain that baby was Mac."

"And if it was?"

Hailey sighed. "If a DNA test proves she's right, then we have to let her see Brady. And Luna, of course."

"What happens from there?" Nick asked softly.

Tears filled her eyes. "We share him. Luna too."

"Oh, Hailey," said Nick. "You're such a wonderful, generous woman. I know this is hard for you for many reasons. But we'll do the right thing together."

Too emotional to speak, Hailey could only nod and lean in against him.

Later, as they checked on the kids in bed, Hailey couldn't help but linger in their rooms. She loved each one, wanted to keep them safe and happy.

Careful not to wake him, Hailey planted a whisper of a kiss on Brady's cheek and did the same for the girls. Time would take care of her worries.

The next day, a report from the detective confirmed a lot of what Missy had told them and more. Wallace Linley was a successful but temperamental man who was used to being in control and obeyed. A typical New York, powerful, big-time operator. He'd met Missy after she'd come to New York to try her success with modeling agencies. Against all advice and former determination to appear as socially acceptable as possible, Wallace told friends he was beguiled by the young waitress he met at a cocktail party a fellow businessman had for friends and prospective clients and that he intended to marry her.

Word on the street was Wallace pursued Missy until she couldn't say no. Missy was an attractive hostess for him, and while she was well-liked, her husband wasn't always highly regarded.

Hailey stopped reading and shook her head. It was worse than a soap opera.

The detective had found a birth certificate in Westchester records for a baby boy called Henry Macklin, no known father.

Slowly, the pieces of the puzzle were coming together. The people who adopted Henry were named MacGrath. But instead of providing a good life and a solid upbringing to him, the MacGraths were cited by the state for child neglect, and Henry "Mac" was placed in foster care, which is where he met Linnie.

Such a tragedy thought Hailey.

During the next week, Hailey and Nick met with Owen to discuss what to do next.

"I don't want Brady exposed to Wallace Linley," said Hailey. "I have bad vibes about him."

Owen nodded. "My understanding is that at this point, Wallace is unaware of the world around him but lives in the past when he's somewhat lucid."

"I don't want Missy to have free rein with Brady. If the DNA test, which we've agreed to, shows a connection, Missy is not to be with Brady without the presence of either Hailey or me," said Nick.

"I agree. Furthermore, you will dictate times together, not she," said Owen. "Missy has agreed to meet with your friend, Dr. Mike Garrett, if any issues come up for Brady."

"We've talked about Brady," said Hailey. "Does she realize Luna might be her grandchild too?"

"Yes," said Owen, "In further discussions, I've told her, but we're taking it one step at a time. We'll start with Brady and see how things go. I wouldn't agree to her seeing Brady or meeting with you if I didn't believe her story. We have facts, but more than that, I've been able to talk to Missy and visit with her in person when she's been in the area. Are you aware she's house hunting here?"

"No, I'm not," Hailey said. "Does she know she can't intrude? I don't want her thinking she can barge into our lives."

Nick placed a hand on Hailey's arm. "We won't let that happen."

"I know." Hailey sank her head into her hands and drew a deep breath. When she lifted her face, she felt more confident. "I'm sorry. I have many mixed emotions when it comes to this. But I also sympathize with Missy. Once we get proof from the DNA test, we can decide what to do."

"Exactly," said Owen. "You've already provided a sample from Brady?"

"Last week," said Nick. "They're going to try to rush it through. Missy provided a fresh sample just a day or two earlier."

"Then it's out of our hands," said Owen. "But I truly believe we already have our answer. In this state, grandparents have rights. I'm glad we're settling this amicably. We certainly wouldn't want to fight this out in court."

"Heavens no," said Hailey. "It just seems very strange that this has happened. It scares me a bit."

"Understandably," said Owen. "But in this case, you have several people working for you who will see that it isn't scary for anyone."

"We appreciate your support," said Nick. "As you can imagine we want only what's best for our family."

It wasn't a big surprise when two weeks later the DNA report came back concluding Missy and Brady shared a definite connection. They hadn't bothered to have Luna tested, but Missy was now tied to her, too.

CHAPTER 6

As agreed, on a Wednesday morning, Hailey met Missy at Gracie's restaurant at the Salty Key Inn for a late breakfast when the kids were in school. Missy was staying at the hotel while she looked for housing in the area.

Hailey, too nervous to wait, arrived early and took a seat at a table facing the entrance. As Hailey sipped a cup of coffee, she thought of Missy and wondered if Missy was feeling as awkward and fragile.

A few minutes later, Hailey had her answer when Missy walked into the restaurant and seeing Hailey, her face crumpled. With dignity, she walked to the table even as tears escaped her eyes.

On autopilot, Hailey stood and reached for her. Exchanging hugs, Hailey felt tears of her own. "Hello, Missy," she managed to say. "I'm glad we could meet and start the process of getting to know one another."

"Me, too," said Missy, taking a seat opposite Hailey.

Hailey cleared her throat. "We haven't mentioned

you or your name to Brady, but we'll begin to do that in the coming days. First, I need to get to know you better."

"Oh, yes, I understand," said Missy. "I don't want to burst on the scene, but rather hope to be more and more included as you allow." She stopped and stared into space before turning back to Hailey. "You can't imagine what finding Brady means to me. You're a mother yourself so you can understand how devastated I was at the way things happened after I gave birth to his father. A mother never forgets her child."

Hailey nodded. "I have three children, not just one. Each is precious to me."

"Yes, I understand. Your lawyer told me that in addition to Brady, I have a granddaughter, Luna. It's like a miracle. I can't wait to meet her too."

Hailey studied Missy. "Actually, Luna favors you. Her eyes and nose are a bit like yours."

A huge smile spread across Missy's face. "Really?" she whispered. "That's wonderful. You can't know how happy that makes me."

"Both Brady and Luna are special children—bright, kind, and loving."

"I understand you and Nick are great parents," Missy said, giving her a look of approval that Hailey appreciated.

"We try," said Hailey. "I know you and Wallace had no children. He was older when you married him. Did he have children of his own?"

"No," said Missy crisply. "He didn't want them. And then we found out he wasn't able to have them.

Wallace ... well, he could sometimes be a headstrong man."

"But you made the marriage work," said Hailey.

"Yes, we made that commitment to each other," said Missy. "And until the past few years, I was able to help him with his business. Now, of course, the business has sold, and the man I married has disappeared into a world of his own. As sad as it may sound, the changes in our lives allowed me to pursue my dream of finding my son. I had no idea Mac MacGrath was mine until I saw the photograph of Brady. I did some research of my own with the help of a detective." Missy reached across the table and squeezed Hailey's hand. "I wouldn't have disturbed you if I hadn't been sure, myself, about what I suspected."

"It was quite a shock, as you can imagine," said Hailey. "But I consider it an opportunity for both the kids and you to have a connection. I just want it done in such a way that it seems natural. Luna has no recollection of her birth parents, but Brady remembers them both."

"I see," said Missy agreeably. She leaned forward. "Now, tell me a little about you. I've read several of your books. They're lovely treasures. I've donated hundreds of copies to hospitals in the city."

"Thank you. That means a lot to me. I've always been a reader. My adoptive mother used to read to my sister and me every night, letting me dream about and learn new things. I now use words and pictures to tell stories of my own." Hailey smiled. "Luna loves to tell stories, and April loves to draw."

"Tell me more about the children," said Missy, her eyes aglow.

"I'll start with Brady. You know he's musical and talented. Nick insists he take piano lessons though he personally gives Brady guitar lessons. They have a strong bond between them, strengthened, of course, by their love of music. Brady is a gentle, kind soul. His mother, Linnie, told him to take care of his sister when Luna was born, and he's always taken that role seriously with both girls. You know from photographs that he has a strong resemblance to his grandfather."

Missy nodded and brushed tears from her cheeks. "His grandfather was smart. Top of his class. The only way I graduated high school was through GED courses. Things are very different today. I would've had a better chance of being open and honest in our present-day environment. But then it was impossible, and I didn't want to ruin Henry's life. With this new knowledge about Mac, I'm working to let go of the past and move ahead in a way I've been unable to for years."

"What is it you want from Brady? Luna? Us?" Hailey asked, speaking boldly.

"I want the chance to get to know you, spend what time I can with you, to help me realize that the love I shared with someone was meaningful and lives on today."

Hailey was quiet, letting those thoughts settle in her head.

"I know you need time to get to know me, to permit me into your lives. I understand that. I've waited over forty years. I'll try to be patient."

"What ever happened to your Henry?"

"A terrible hunting accident," said Missy. "My life was bad after I had the baby. And then, when I heard Henry had been killed, I closed down completely. I made my way to New York City. The rest is history."

"I'm sorry," said Hailey. "Your story has made me wonder about my own life. I was taken into foster care by a woman who later died of a drug overdose. That's all I know. At eight, I was brought into another foster home by a wonderful woman who adopted me. I was lucky."

"And so are Brady and Luna," said Missy giving Hailey a steady look.

"Thank you," Hailey said, becoming more optimistic about the future. Maybe, as she'd done with Maddie, she could be friends with Missy.

Before they left the restaurant, Hailey took photographs of Missy to show the children when it was time. She couldn't help admiring the pictures she'd taken of Missy. She was a beautiful woman.

They agreed to introduce the children to Missy slowly, maybe adding photographs as a way to talk about her to make sure they all would feel comfortable. First, Missy, would have dinner with Nick and Hailey. Nick wanted to have the chance to get to know her better.

After talking it over, Nick and Hailey decided to make their dinner date with Missy a casual one and to include Mike and Janna. Nick wanted to see how flexible Missy was about dealing with a change of plans, and Hailey wanted Mike's input after meeting Missy.

They set up a time to meet at the Pink Pelican, a casual beach bar and restaurant not far from them. They made reservations early so they wouldn't collide with the younger crowd who'd be rocking to a band's music later on.

When Hailey and Nick arrived at the restaurant, Mike and Janna were already seated at a table for six out on the wooden deck. As they were being seated, Missy arrived. In her fifties and wearing a simple sundress, Missy looked fabulous, somewhat like Naomi Watts.

She shook hands with Mike and Janna and took a seat next to Hailey. "This is a lovely setting," she said smiling. "I'm glad I could join you. I'll be heading back to New York for a couple of days and will return for several weeks. I've found a house I want to buy and can't wait to work out the details."

"Congratulations. Where is your new house located?" Janna asked.

"In St. Petersburg. In Snell Isle," Missy said. "I was thrilled to find it."

"That's a lovely area," said Hailey. "How nice." Million dollar homes were part of it.

"As long as Wallace is alive, I'll have to travel back and forth. Most of the time he has no idea who I am, but, occasionally he does, and that's important to me. When I married Wallace, I made a commitment to him. He's much older than I am. Almost fifteen years."

The appearance of the waitress stopped their conversation.

After ordering, Missy turned to Janna. "I understand you and Hailey are close friends."

Janna grinned. "Yes, we clicked right away. We've been even closer ever since. Hailey is the person who made sure I met Mike."

"Mike's daughter, Zoe, is Brady's age. They're best friends," said Hailey. "And Nick and Mike both teach at the University of South Florida in Tampa. Mike in the psychology department and Nick in the music department."

"Yes, I do know that," said Missy with a twinkle in her eye. "I am as curious about you as I'm sure you're curious about me."

Mike laughed. "Let's say we all want to get to know one another. Yours is an unusual story. Hailey and Nick have filled me in on it so I'm able to assess Brady's reaction to the news of an unexpected grandmother in his life."

Missy nodded. "That sounds only fair." Her eyes suddenly swam with tears. "It means more than you know for me to have found my grandchildren and with such wonderful people. If only I'd been able to find out about my son earlier. I tried, but with the name change and a totally unsuspected change in location, I couldn't trace him."

"And you didn't want your husband to know," Hailey said quietly.

"True. Ours was and is an unusual relationship. He offered a life many dream of, and I suppose it was survival for me, and a bit of ego for him."

"What questions do you have for us?" Nick asked. "We've certainly been asking a lot about you, and you've been very forthright."

"Hailey told me she never met Mac, but became

friends with Linnie. I know he turned himself around from a drug addiction. He was also active in charity work in Florida. Do either of you have any personal knowledge of him?"

"I watched him play on television a number of times and once saw him play in person," said Nick. "He was well-respected by the other players, which means a lot."

"I agree," said Mike. "He was approachable with fans, and when news broadcasters spoke sadly of his death, they meant it."

"Thank you," said Missy. "I like to think he was a fine young man. His father was a great guy."

Their food and drinks came, and their conversation turned to the house Missy had bought and different places she might want to visit in the area.

By the time their meal was finished and a band was setting up, Hailey realized she really liked Missy. She might be part of a high society group in New York, but here in Florida, she was down-to-earth. More than that, she thought she and Missy might actually become friends one day—as long as she wasn't intrusive with the children.

On the way home, Hailey said, "What do you think of Missy?"

Nick smiled and nodded. "If we had to have a surprise grandmother, she isn't bad at all. We'll be careful with her meeting the kids and spending time with her. Then we'll have a better idea how it's all going to work out."

"I agree," said Hailey. "One day, one step at a time. Like Owen says, she needs the chance to at least meet the kids."

"Yes, that's how we'll play it. Such an odd circumstance, but we've learned life is full of surprises." He gave her a teasing look. "Who knew that a shy little sister of a classmate would end up being my wife?"

Hailey laughed. She'd had a crush on him as a teenager.

Later, when Missy called to say goodbye, Hailey suggested that if she was back in Florida in time for Halloween, Missy could join them for a neighborhood party for the kids. "That way, we can keep your first meeting with them low-key. You'll just be part of the adults. How does that sound?"

"Like something we all can easily handle. Much better than making a big appearance that might be confusing."

"Exactly," said Hailey pleased. She still had concerns about things happening too fast. If they introduced Missy in their lives, she didn't want the kids to suffer any loss if things didn't work out.

CHAPTER 7

Hailey loved Halloween. It was a reason for kids to use their imaginations to come up with costume ideas. She wasn't a seamstress but could manage a few simple costumes if necessary.

The girls were easy. Fairies, angels, or princesses would do nicely. Brady was a different story. He went from wanting to dress up as a football player, to a violinist, to Spiderman. After much indecision, he decided to be a football player.

Though they had Halloween parties at school, the kids' favorite celebration was the annual neighborhood party which took place in one of the twenty houses in Nick and Hailey's small area. This year, their next-door neighbor was hosting the party. It would be held outside, as usual, allowing the annual treasure hunt to take place.

Hailey had arranged for Missy to come to their house. From there, they'd join the party.

When Missy showed up wearing a tiara, Hailey laughed out loud. "You'll fit right in with the girls."

Hailey watched as Zeke sniffed Missy and then wagged his tail and licked the hand she held out to him. Dogs were exceptional judges of people, and Missy had passed his test. Pleased, Hailey said, "Come on inside."

"Who's there?" Luna asked, approaching them wearing a silky blue princess outfit and a sparkly tiara. She stared up at Missy's head. "You're a princess too? Like me."

"Luna, please say hello to Miss … Miss Missy …" Hailey stuttered over the name, unsure.

"Missy?" said Luna.

"Why don't we make it easy and simply let the kids call me Missy," Missy suggested. "A new beginning for me."

"Great idea," said Hailey. She wasn't quite ready for the kids to call Missy grandma. That was Maddie's name.

"Watch," said Luna, twirling around in circles and waving a wand. "I'm dancing."

"I like to dance too," said Missy looking on.

April came running over to them. "Mommy, Luna took my wand. I want it back."

"I can't find mine," said Luna, pulling the wand close to her. "I want hers."

"Luna, you need to give April her wand. I'll help you find yours," said Hailey, hoping the spat would be over soon. Halloween evenings could be tough. She tried to limit sugary treats, but it was one day of the year when it was more difficult than most.

Brady walked over to them, wearing his football uniform.

Missy's face turned white and then reddened as she managed a friendly expression.

Hailey put an arm around Brady. "I'd like you to meet someone special. Miss Missy, but we're calling her Missy."

Brady held out his hand as he'd been taught.

Missy took hold of it and shook it, beaming at him. "You look so much like a dear old friend of mine. I'm very pleased to meet you."

He nodded, studied Missy's tiara, and turned to Hailey. "Can you help me? I want to put on my shoulder pads. They make me look bigger."

"Sure," said Hailey. "Let me help Luna find her wand and then I'll see what I can do."

"That's okay. Dad can do it. He said he and I can walk over to the Pierces' together. He's ready now."

"Okay. We'll catch up to you." Hailey waved for Missy to follow her, certain she would love seeing the girls' room.

It was like a fairyland with white poster beds, pink bedspreads, dolls, and princess items everywhere. Little fairies danced on one wall painted pink. The rest of the walls were an even paler pink. Hailey knew she'd over-done it with the decorating, but she and the girls loved the room.

"Ah, how pretty," gushed Missy when she followed Hailey inside.

Luna took hold of Missy's hand. "Come see my animals. I've got lots of them."

Missy laughed. "I see that. Have you found your

wand?"

Luna shook her head. "I think Zeke took it."

"Let's see, shall we?" said Hailey. When she was frustrated, Luna tended to blame things on Zeke, who was often guilty of her accusations.

April crawled under the flounce of the bed ruffle on Luna's bed and emerged a moment later holding the wand. "Here it is."

"Thank you," Hailey said to her. "Okay, Luna, give April her wand and thank her for finding yours."

Luna sighed and dramatically placed a hand on her hip. "Thanks, Sissy."

Hailey exchanged amused glances with Missy as the two girls switched wands. "Okay, my little princesses. Let's go to the party."

Their argument forgotten, Luna and April left the room together.

"They're adorable," said Missy following Hailey out of the room. "I do see similarities between Luna and me."

"Me, too," said Hailey. "Her spunk reminds me of Linnie, but I suspect some of that came from you too."

Missy clasped her hands together. "This, being here with you and them is like a dream come true. Sometimes I have to pinch myself to make sure it's real. Thank you, Hailey, for allowing me to spend time with them."

"You're welcome. Let's enjoy the evening. I think you'll like our neighbors. It's a congenial group."

"How will you introduce me?" Missy said.

Hailey paused. "How about a special friend of the family?"

Missy smiled and nodded. "Okay, that sounds fine. I don't want to intrude."

"Thank you." Hailey returned Missy's smile. "Let's have fun before all the kids have sugar-induced meltdowns."

That night, after Missy left and the kids were tucked into bed, Hailey sank onto a couch in the living room exhausted. It had been an emotional day. She liked Missy, liked how considerate Missy was of Hailey's protectiveness, but she wasn't used to the idea of sharing her children with anyone outside her small circle of friends.

Nick came and sat beside her. "Halloween is always fun for the kids, but it's nice when they finally settle down. I thought Missy handled them well, especially when the bickering began."

Hailey nodded. "Me, too. I invited her to join us for April's birthday. And she was very pleased."

"That's generous of you, Hailey." He drew her to him and kissed her on the lips.

Fatigue melted away as his kiss deepened.

A few days later, Hailey was surprised by a phone call from Missy. Smiling, she picked it up. "Hi, Missy. What's up?"

"I'm afraid I won't be able to make April's birthday party."

"Oka-a-ay," Hailey said, wondering if this was the kind of unreliable relationship it would be for the kids. Maddie's mother, Nan, had always been there for her was another source of security.

Missy continued. "I need to tell you something before you see it on television or hear about it elsewhere. When Wallace sold his business, he and his partner had a major disagreement about how the proceeds from the sale were to be divided. I thought it was all settled. Now his partner is suing Wallace for millions of dollars claiming all kinds of things. Wallace, of course, is unable to be of much help to our lawyers. While I have no knowledge of what agreements were in place, his partner is including me in the lawsuit."

Hailey couldn't hold back a gasp. "That's awful!" She remembered the detective she'd hired to find out about Missy had mentioned a problem between Wallace and his partner, but she, too, thought it had been settled.

"I want you to know I was not a part of Wallace's actions. It's important for me to be totally honest with you considering our new connection. My lawyer has indicated there are enough problematic issues that, at the very best, I'll lose the penthouse I live in. Though I can no longer go through with the purchase of the house in Snell Isle, he told me I should go ahead and find a smaller place to live in Florida, away from the circus that has already started around this case. Wallace was a very tough businessman, not well-liked. Some people are rejoicing over this action, telling everyone they know that he deserves this."

"How terrible! What about you? How can I help?"

Hailey asked, feeling sick to her stomach.

"I know how concerned you are about any publicity concerning your children. So, I'm not asking for anything from you except to believe me. I promise I had no knowledge of details or participation in the sale of the business. My lawyer knows that. Right now, I'm following his instructions by marking certain things in my home that I want to keep, hoping I'll be allowed to do so. I'll drive to Florida and buy a small place in the area so I have somewhere to live. No reasonable judge or jury would deny me that."

"What about things like jewelry and clothes?" Hailey asked.

"My housekeeper and I have already begun to pack some clothes and personal items. That's something you can help me with. May I have some boxes shipped to you?"

"How about shipping them to me at the library?" said Hailey, thinking quickly. "They'll be safe there, and that makes it clear I have no knowledge of what's inside. Make sure that's approved by your lawyer."

Hailey heard quiet sobbing. When she spoke, Missy's voice was wobbly. "Thank you, Hailey. You have no idea what that means to me. All the women who I thought were my friends have deserted me or called just to get some information out of me. I've never felt so alone. Well, maybe one other time ..." her voice drifted away.

"Where are you going to stay in Florida while you search for a new home?" Hailey asked.

"I think I'll return to the Salty Key Inn. It's a lovely, quiet property."

"And close enough to Janna and me for us to be able to help you," said Hailey with fresh determination. After all the research they'd done on Missy's character and her background, and after meeting her, Hailey felt confident that helping her was the right thing to do. Still, she needed Nick's agreement to do anything beyond having packages sent to the library.

"I hope you understand Nick will want to speak to your lawyer. Please give me his name and number," said Hailey. "We're here to support you, Missy, but need to know how best to provide help."

"I appreciate it."

Hailey wrote down the information Missy gave her and said, "What else can I do?"

"I don't want to intrude and definitely don't want this to affect the kids in any way," said Missy. Her voice broke. "I thought for the first time in my life that happy news was truly mine."

"I'd be glad to look at any houses you want me to," said Hailey. "It sounds as if it's going to take you some time to get here."

"That would be lovely," said Missy. "My next call is to the real estate agent. She'll be as disappointed as I am about the house I'd picked out and now can't have. But I think my lawyer is right. I can't be seen living in a fancy place if we lose the case. I know now that his partner will take whatever he can from me. He's made that very clear, complaining that he was never given fair credit for building the business. I'll get back to you after I talk to the agent."

"What about Wallace?" Hailey asked.

"Those funds are protected. We've signed a contract

71

with the facility where he's living. That will stay in place."

"What if you win the case?" Hailey asked, forcing optimism into her voice.

"Whenever I've asked that, my lawyer has shaken his head. Apparently, there's going to be some loss no matter what. He's just trying to protect what personal items of mine he can for me. I'm not sorry to leave New York after finding you. And I'm healthy enough to work if that becomes necessary. That's what I have to keep in mind."

"I'm very sorry this has happened to you," said Hailey. "This will weigh heavily on my mind. Please keep in touch."

"I will," said Missy. "Thank you for being as sweet as you are. If you change your mind in the future about staying in touch with me, I'll understand. Whether it's right or not, my reputation will be pretty much ruined when this all comes out. I'd better go. Goodbye."

"Take care," said Hailey, stunned by this new information. She wasn't so naïve that she didn't believe such things happened, but it bothered her that Missy would have to suffer because of her husband's actions. She punched in Nick's number and caught him between classes.

After she explained what was going on, Hailey said, We have to help Missy."

"Hold on," said Nick. "There's a lot more we need to know. I'll call her lawyer and talk to him."

"Okay," said Hailey, but she already knew that unless it was very bad information about Missy, she wanted to help her.

CHAPTER 8

When a text came from Missy giving her the name of the real estate agent who'd been helping her, Hailey called the company. This was something she could do for Missy without getting too entangled.

Margaret Clinton-Dewar answered her call with a crisp, "Hello."

Hailey explained who she was and asked if they could meet.

"Yes, of course. I just got off a call with Missy. She's such a lovely person and certainly doesn't deserve to be embroiled in a situation like hers. She knows I've been caught in a similar situation—to a much lesser degree, which is why I divorced my first husband. I'm more than ready to help her."

"Did she tell you of our connection?" asked Hailey, curious to see if Missy was being discreet.

"Missy said you're a new friend made through mutual acquaintances, but she trusts you to help her.

For a woman in her position to be able to say that means quite a bit. I understand the need to find something suitable quickly and welcome your input. Missy loves your taste."

Pleased, Hailey said, "I can meet you right away. I'll hire a sitter to pick up the girls from preschool and for my son when he gets out of school." She blessed Nick for coming up with the arrangement with Taylor.

"I'll line up a number of homes for you to look at online before actually visiting any. And then sometimes a drive through the neighborhood is enough to help narrow down choices for Missy to consider."

"I'll call you back in a few minutes after making sure I've got a sitter lined up for the kids." Hailey ended the call and placed one to Taylor. With everything set, Hailey changed her clothes and left the house, eager to help.

Margaret was an attractive woman with dark-brown, shoulder-length hair and light-brown eyes that lit when she smiled. Hailey immediately felt comfortable with her. Dressed in a brown-linen sheath that fit her trim body and wearing a simple pearl necklace that matched her earrings, Margaret looked as professional as she'd sounded.

"It's a pleasure to meet you," Margaret said. "I already have some houses for you to look at, including one just down the coast from your house. Missy mentioned she wanted to stay in this general area."

"I've seen pictures of the house Missy wanted to buy in Snell Isle. It was stunning. Palatial actually."

"Yes, it was a beautiful home. We're looking for

something simpler now," said Margaret with a note of regret. "But I'm going to try my best to please her."

"Me, too," said Hailey, following Margaret into her office.

"Care for a bottle of cold water or a soda?" Margaret asked.

"No thanks. I'm excited to see what you've come up with," said Hailey, taking a seat in a chair in front of Margaret's desk and staring at a computer screen swiveled to face her.

The houses that Margaret showed her online all held promise. Even though they were far less expensive than the house Missy had originally selected, they were in a price range that was higher than Hailey had expected.

Margaret explained what was on Missy's list of necessities, and they compared those qualities with each house. They marked locations, the pluses and minuses of each, and selected three properties to tour in person.

One of the classes Hailey had taken in college was home design, and she loved viewing other people's homes. This was even more exciting because she knew of Missy's need to move quickly.

While she was in the car with Margaret on their way to tour the first house, Hailey's phone rang. *Nick.*

"Hi," she said, clicking on the call.

"Hi," said Nick. "I was able to talk to Missy's lawyer. It seems this is one of those cases where the press is going to try to play up every detail. Wallace Linley wasn't that nice a guy when it came to business, and he made some enemies in the city who are more than happy to see things go bad for him. Unfortunately,

Missy's name will be caught up in the mess. It might be best if we just step aside for the moment."

Hailey let out a long sigh. She and Nick rarely argued, but there was no way she'd "step aside for the moment." She paused and said, "We'll talk later tonight."

She ended the call and stared out the window.

"Everything all right?" Margaret asked.

Hailey nodded, but knew it wasn't. She was used to being very open with Nick about things. It bothered her that she was doing something he might not like, but she felt strongly that this was the right thing to do.

Later, after touring their three favorite homes, she and Margaret agreed that only one of them was worth considering. A cash payment meant flexibility in price, and Margaret intended to make an offer that would please Missy the moment she got approval from her.

It was almost suppertime when they returned to the office.

"Can I buy you dinner?" said Margaret.

Hailey shook her head. "Thanks, but I have to get home to the kids." She didn't mention the need to talk to Nick. "Let me know what Missy thinks about our choice for her. I love the house, and the location is great."

"I agree," said Margaret smiling. "Thank you for your input. You said you're going to text Missy with pictures. I'll do the same. It would be wonderful if we could get this deal to go through this week."

"I hope it does," said Hailey. "Very nice meeting you. Missy is lucky to have found you."

"Thanks," said Margaret. "Here's my card. Call with any questions or thoughts you might have."

Hailey left Margaret's office with a sense of satisfaction. They'd done their best for Missy.

Hailey arrived home to find Taylor serving dinner to the children in the kitchen.

"Where's Nick?" Hailey asked before she went to the kitchen table to greet her children.

"He called to say he'd be late. He asked where you were, and I told him you had an appointment with a real estate agent."

Hailey wished she'd had a chance to tell him first. She bent to kiss each child, thankful as always for their happy smiles to see her.

"How was school today?" Hailey asked.

"I learned my A's," said April.

"I already know the whole alphabet," said Luna proudly.

"Can you help me with my homework?" Brady said. "I have to write a story."

"Sure," said Hailey. "All you need is a beginning, middle, and end." She grinned saying the words. Stories at any level were much more than that. Picture books like she wrote were as difficult as any.

While the children continued eating, Hailey caught up with Taylor and asked if she'd be available later in the week. "I'm not sure when I'll need you. I just need to know you can be flexible."

"Absolutely," said Taylor. "You know I love being here with the kids."

Hailey gave her a hug. "Thanks. You're the best." She bid Taylor goodbye and went back to the kitchen.

After dinner, the girls settled in front of the television with a taped educational show they loved, and Hailey sat at the kitchen table with Brady. She loved the ability to talk to him without the competition for attention from his sisters. He was a quiet child but full of ideas.

"What do you have to write about?" Hailey asked him.

"My favorite thing to do," Brady replied.

"You have many things you like to do. Which one are you going to pick?" she asked, certain it would have something to do with music.

"Building sandcastles," he said, surprising her.

"Okay, what else did the teacher tell you?"

"She said I have to tell why I like doing that," said Brady.

"Do you know the answer to that?" she asked gently.

Brady nodded. "It's for our family. I like that."

"And friends, too," she reminded him.

"Yes. Are we going to put Missy inside?" he asked. Sandcastles were temporary homes for the people they loved. Placing someone inside, using stick figures, was an affirmation of affection and love for that individual. It was how Hailey had helped Brady keep his family close in spirit.

"We can add Missy next time we make one. Would you like that?" Hailey asked, again surprised by him.

"Yes. She wants to be there," said Brady. "I just know it."

"Then, the next time we build a sandcastle, we'll include her," said Hailey, her eyes stinging with tears. Missy would be thrilled to know he wanted her to be part of it.

"All right. Put down your thoughts, and I can check it for you," said Hailey. Brady was in an advanced class, and she was anxious to see what he would say. At his age, it would be simple but meaningful.

Brady was working on his assignment when Nick walked inside.

"Hello, everyone, I'm home," he called. As he kissed Hailey, the girls rushed into the kitchen to give him hugs. And then it was Brady's turn.

"What'cha doing, bud?" he asked, giving Brady a loving pat on the shoulder.

"Writing a story," said Brady proudly.

"I thought maybe we could talk while the kids are busy, and then we can have a light supper," said Hailey. "Sound okay?"

"Great," said Nick. "Lots to talk about."

"Yes," said Hailey, giving him a steady look. "Brady wants to include Missy in our sandcastles."

Nick's eyebrows shot up with surprise. "Let me change my clothes, and I'll meet you on the lanai."

After Nick left the kitchen, Hailey poured glasses of iced tea and fixed a plate of cheese and crackers to take outside with her.

Smelling the cheese, the dogs, followed her.

While waiting for Nick, Hailey looked out at the water, staring at the movement of the waves rushing to shore and pulling back again like a shy child. She thought of Brady's remark about Missy and felt a lump form in her throat. Children saw and understood much more than people gave them credit for. He'd obviously seen the need inside Missy.

Lost in thought, Hailey startled when Nick placed a hand on her shoulder and sat in a chair beside her.

"Busy day?" she asked him. Though Nick worked some evenings with his band, he was usually home by late afternoon. He'd planned his schedule that way so he could have time with the kids.

"Yes, as a matter of fact it was. After talking to Missy's lawyer, I did some investigation of my own. Wallace Linley was an extremely wealthy man at one point. Over the past several years, he and his partner lost clients, and word on the street was that they both were glad to sell the company. Wallace was getting sick, and his partner, Sydney Rubin, didn't have the knowledge to run it alone. It's one of those public disputes the press loves."

"Yes," said Hailey. "That's why it's unfair to Missy to be brought into it. Her lawyer is trying to protect her, but, apparently, there are enough questions that he's afraid there's reason for her to suffer a huge financial loss."

"It's one thing for you to help by allowing Missy to ship boxes to you, but I think we shouldn't get too involved. We don't know Missy that well, and it's a messy situation." Nick shifted in his seat. "I know you have good intentions but ..."

"I'm doing more for her," Hailey said, cutting him off. "I'm helping her find a house in the area. Her lawyer said it would be a bad idea for her to go through with the purchase of the house in Snell Isle. I'm working with her real estate agent on finding another home."

"But you and I agreed we'd talk tonight," Nick said.

"I know, but this opportunity came up, and I'm willing to help," said Hailey. She spoke quietly but with a new sense of purpose. It wasn't right that Missy become a part of something so ugly because she was married to a powerful man who had made some enemies. Missy seemed a decent person who hadn't harmed anyone. She wasn't the first woman to be hurt because of her husband's behavior. And in an arena of big money she wouldn't be the last.

"Could we at least agree not to go further until we see how things develop?" said Nick.

"Let me think about it. This situation has brought back a lot of feelings, and I need time to work through them," Hailey said quietly.

Nick nodded. "Let's set it aside for now. I heard from the record company. They want Brady and me to send them a demo. I thought we could work on that this weekend."

"That should be fine. The girls have a birthday party to go to on Saturday. Otherwise, no activities. Not yet."

Later, as they got ready for bed, Nick studied her. "Are you all right?"

Hailey nodded, but she knew she wasn't. She had a lot on her mind.

CHAPTER 9

Hailey awoke feeling as if she'd been swimming upstream in a raging river. Her body ached from her restlessness, and though her head felt fuzzy, her mind was clear. All night she'd had dreams from childhood. Though she knew they weren't true, she couldn't shake the feeling of despair that she'd felt as a young, confused, frightened child. It didn't matter how old someone was, their bad experiences were tucked inside of them. You never forgot. They shaped who they were and decisions they made. The same was as true for Missy as it was for her. Survival was a strong instinct.

Nick slept soundly beside her as she stared up at the ceiling fan turning slowly above her. Hailey's life had turned out well because one woman was willing to reach out to her. Hailey knew she had to do the same for someone else even if it meant conflict in her own home. She wanted to protect the children, and she would. But they also needed to know the value of helping someone. Brady had already seen the vulnerability in Missy.

Nick stirred.

She rolled over and reached for him.

He drew her close and kissed her. "Hello."

She smiled. "Good morning to you. I'm going to fix you something special for breakfast today, and then we need to talk."

His gaze reached inside her. "You've made a decision then."

"Yes," she said. "And it's going to be all right."

"Whatever it is, we'll do it together," said Nick. "I trust you."

She smiled at him. "Do you know how much I love you?"

"Yeah," he said grinning at her. "Love you too."

Hailey got out of bed, slipped on some clothes, and headed down to the kitchen. She had some time before the children had to get up, and she was going to put it to good use. Blueberry muffins were Nick's favorite.

As she mixed the ingredients, Hailey's lips curved at the memory of the first time she'd made them for him. It was after their first argument—something silly about paint color in one of the rooms in the condo in Granite Ridge. Warm blueberry muffins had softened both their stances, and sitting there together at the breakfast table had made a compromise easy.

Brady walked into the room. "Smells yum, Mom." He poured himself some orange juice and sat at the kitchen counter watching her. She studied his sweet face, seeing both Linnie and his father in his features. She realized what a miracle it was for Missy to discover her grandchildren. It was as if fate had repaid her for the way she'd been treated when she had Brady's father.

Nick came into the kitchen and wrapped his arms around Hailey. "This usually means a compromise. Will we have time to talk about it?"

"Sure. You don't have to go into Tampa until late today. Right?"

He nodded. "I don't like to have things unsettled between us." He kissed her and turned to Brady. "This afternoon, I'll pick you up at school, and we'll drive together into Tampa to the studio. The record company wants a demo from us. Pretty exciting stuff."

A huge smile spread across Brady's face. "Okay."

The quiet morning moment was shattered with the arrival of the girls. Listening to them chatting away to one another, Hailey was reminded of her childhood with three sisters. Girls always seemed to have something to talk about.

After getting the girls to preschool and seeing that Brady was on the bus, Hailey headed home eager to talk to Nick. She'd made a decision and needed him to agree to it.

He was waiting for her in the kitchen when she returned. "Fresh coffee?" he asked her.

She smiled her thanks and accepted a cup from him. "Ready to talk?"

"Yes, I was awake a lot of the night thinking of my mother."

"Your mother?" she asked, surprised.

He nodded. "You remember how Mom was, right? The candy store in Granite Ridge was a success not because of the wonderful chocolates and other candy, but because my mother was one of the kindest, most thoughtful people I've ever known." He smiled at her. "You're so much like her in that way."

"Did you know your mother made me believe for a while that my glasses were magical because I could see things that others might miss?" Hailey shook her head. "She was always doing something nice for others."

"Yeah. My sister is doing a great job of carrying on the tradition, but I still miss Mom."

"Stacy is the one who encouraged me to believe that you might have an interest in me after you first came back to Granite Ridge. Did you know that?"

Nick chuckled. "No, but it sounds just like my sister. She thought we'd be great together from the beginning." His expression sobered. "I've been thinking we should ask Missy to stay with us for a while, away from any possible infringement of her privacy."

Hailey couldn't hold back a squeal of excitement as she set down her coffee cup and threw herself into Nick's arms. "But that's what I was going to talk to you about. Oh, Nick, do you have any idea how much I love you?"

He grinned. "I'm not sure, but I think it's just gone up a level."

Hailey laughed. "And how. I thought about Missy all night and knew we had to do something more for her. While you thought of your mother, I thought of Maddie taking me in. I felt as hopeless as Missy sounded. She's been looking for her son all these years, and now that she's found us, we can't let her down."

"I agree. We've done enough research to know she's a decent person. The kids are already happy to have her near, and we can deal with any repercussions if they arise."

"Let's call her right now," said Hailey.

The person who answered the phone said, "The Linley residence."

"May I please speak to Missy," said Hailey. After a long pause, Hailey added, "Tell her it's Hailey."

Moments later, Missy spoke in a tentative voice. "Hi, Hailey. How are you?"

"I'm feeling much better. You're on speakerphone. Nick and I have talked, and we are inviting you to stay with us until you can get settled in a house. That way, your chance for privacy will be much better. We know you need family around you."

Missy was quiet and then she said, "Do you really want to do this? It's very likely that my name will be mentioned with Wallace's, and it won't be good."

Nick spoke quietly but firmly. "We think it's important. The kids will love it, and you need support. Hailey mentioned you're not getting that in New York."

"No," Missy said. "Leaving here won't be difficult. I'll come with the understanding that if it becomes difficult for you, I'll leave. Hopefully, I'll be able to move into a house of my own shortly. I like the house Hailey and Margaret picked out for me. Margaret's working on a deal right now."

"Great," said Hailey. "You don't need to rush into

anything. You've got all the time you need to find the perfect place."

"I … I … can't thank you enough," Missy said, her voice wavering.

"You can store what you need to in our garage," said Nick.

"It won't be much. We want to avoid the accusation that I'm trying to hide assets and keeping the best for myself. I'm only taking what's truly mine from the penthouse. Besides, the Florida lifestyle is very different, and a lot of the furnishings here aren't suitable for there. It'll be a fresh start I hope."

"Let us know when you plan to arrive and if we can do anything else," said Hailey, pleased they could help her.

"Thank you again," Missy said, her voice breaking. "I'll be in touch."

After the call ended, Hailey hugged Nick. "I'm glad we agreed to do this."

"Let's see how it all plays out," said Nick. "It might not be easy."

"I know. I'd better get to work. The deadline for my book is approaching, and you know I don't like to be late."

"I know, Miss Perfectionist," said Nick hugging her.

Hailey laughed. It was true. She wanted her books to be the best they could be, and many illustrations in her books were reiterations of original ones.

Days passed with no word from Missy.

When she finally called one Sunday night, Missy explained, "We've done as much as we could here. Wallace's partner has already listed several paintings he wants if we can't pay him the amount he wants in retribution. The whole deal is getting uglier, and my lawyer is urging me to leave now. The legal issue isn't with me, though it will obviously impact my life."

"Okay, your room is ready. Send us flight information, and we'll have a limo service pick you up at the Tampa International Airport. He'll be holding a sign with the name 'Missy' on it."

"Oh, my! That's so sweet. Thank you. See you tomorrow. I'll text the flight info to you."

Hailey ended the call and sighed. She hoped she and Nick were doing the right thing. It sounded as if things for Missy were even worse.

The next morning, Hailey and Nick sat down with the kids and explained that Missy would be coming to stay in the guest suite for a while.

"She's a very special person to us, especially to you, Brady, and Luna. She's your grandmother, your birth Dad's mother. Do you understand?"

Brady gave her a thoughtful look. "Is she April's grandmother, too?"

"Yes, but in a different way. But all three of you children are precious to her, just like all three of you are precious to Grandma Maddie."

"I love Grandma," said April.

"Grandma loves me," Luna said.

"And now you have a new grandmother to love all of us," said Hailey, seeing the relationship as they might. "This is a stressful time for Missy. Moving from New York to Florida can be hard. We'll need you to be very kind to her."

"Why haven't we met her before?"

Hailey put an arm around him. "Because she didn't know about us until recently."

Brady gave her a puzzled look then nodded.

Hailey looked around at their solemn faces and felt teary. They were so innocent, so concerned.

"Let's think of a nice welcome for her," said Nick. "She'll be here later today."

That afternoon, Hailey stood with Nick and the kids outside, ready to greet Missy. According to Missy, it wouldn't be long until she was ready to move into a home of her own. The purchase of the house Hailey had looked at with Margaret was going through. After repainting and recarpeting the interior, the house would be ready for her. Then the task of furnishing it needed to be accomplished.

"Hi, Missy," cried Luna running forward. "See!" She pointed to the tiara on her head. She stopped and gazed at Missy. "Where's your princess hat?"

Missy smiled. "I'm afraid it's packed up in boxes, but I'll find it one day."

Luna took off her tiara and handed it to Missy. "You can have it for now. I know you're sad."

"I made you a picture," said April, handing Missy a

picture of her standing with the others in front of a house."

Missy's eyes glistened as she embraced Luna and then hugged April who'd followed Luna.

Brady stood by and waited politely for Missy to reach out for him and then allowed a tight hug. "I'm glad you're here. Mom said you're my grandmother."

Missy's eyes widened and then filled with tears. She nodded, too emotional to speak.

Watching her children greet Missy with such warmth brought a smile to Hailey's lips. The joy Missy felt at their welcome was plain to see.

She hugged Missy and watched as Nick did the same. They'd decided if Missy was a family member, she'd be treated that way. Hailey had spent time talking to her mother about it, and Maddie agreed they were doing the right thing.

Brady, carrying one of Missy's smaller bags, headed the procession inside the house.

Hailey proudly showed Missy the guest suite. She knew Missy would be comfortable there. The walls were painted a very pale green exuding a sense of calm to the space. A bright-colored quilt covered the king-size bed and added life to the background. Not only did the room provide privacy away from the kids, but a small, walled patio was protected territory as well. Hailey had always loved that space.

"What can we do to help you get settled?" Hailey asked Missy.

"Nothing, thank you." Missy smiled. "You've done so much for me already. I'll never forget the welcome I got. I'll unpack a bit and change my clothes into something more comfortable."

"Okay. We'll get out of your way for now. If you'd like to take a swim before dinner, the pool is heated. It should be pleasant."

"That sounds delightful," said Missy. "I noticed the kids are in their swimsuits. I think I'll come join you."

As the children left the room, Luna's voice rang out. "Mama, Missy needs a fairy crown."

"I know, sweetheart. We're going to help her find one," Hailey said and then stopped, aware Missy could hear them.

When Missy approached them wearing a bathing suit and carrying a beach towel from her room, Hailey thought she looked more relaxed already.

The children soon had Missy in the pool with them. Hearing their shrieks of laughter as she pretended to chase them, Hailey thought it was sad that Missy had never had the chance to experience life with her own child.

Since meeting Missy, Hailey had tried to do more research on Mac's life. There was a ton of information and stats on his football career, but personal details were few and far between. It was another fact about being in the system that bothered her. It sometimes seemed as if a few kids had no real background at all but had simply existed.

After the kids had tired of the pool and sat on the sidelines, Hailey joined Missy on the steps at the shallow end of the pool. "The kids love having you here. You may regret your decision to stay with us."

Missy chuckled and shook her head. "Not a chance. I live with regrets, but this isn't going to be one of them." She reached over and gave Hailey's hand a squeeze. "I'm very lucky it was you I found. Not many others would give me the same degree of trust that you and Nick have."

"Funny you should say that. We made the decision after thinking about our own mothers. Nick's mother passed away almost six years ago. And my adoptive mother is still alive and very active. But both are examples of the kind of people we want to be."

"That's very sweet. My mother was the opposite for me. I never wanted to be like her. She was not a loving person. She was often emotionally abusive."

"Hey, ladies, how about a refreshing drink to celebrate Missy's arrival?" said Nick.

"A glass of wine sounds nice. How about you, Missy?" said Hailey.

"Perfect. But I don't want to intrude on your special time," Missy said.

"This is a special time for us all," said Nick.

"In the future, you might need to take advantage of your private space," said Hailey. "It's usually pretty hectic around here. I'm sorry you missed April's birthday, but we have Thanksgiving coming up soon. We usually celebrate with Janna and Mike and their kids."

"Sounds like fun. Until recently, of course, Wallace and I usually went out to eat."

"Well, then, you're in for a treat," said Nick. "I do the turkey."

"It's the best," said Hailey.

Missy smiled. "It all sounds wonderful."

Hailey studied her. She wondered what her life with Wallace really was like. A business deal, the press was trying to make it. But Hailey knew it was more than that.

CHAPTER 10

Once the excitement about having a guest in the house wore off, the kids went back to their normal behavior—three kids wanting to be in charge of their own little universe with much-needed interference from adults. Hailey wondered how Missy would handle the change to a more normal situation, but she seemed to roll with it.

Over the course of the next few days, things settled into a comfortable routine with Missy busy dealing with her new house while the rest of them continued with their activities. Hailey tried not to pry, but she was, of course, curious about Missy's reactions to reports coming from New York. As her lawyer had warned, Missy's name came up. As often happens when someone is being blamed for things, old friends either stepped away from Missy or tore her down.

"How are you?" Hailey asked Missy one afternoon when they were alone.

"Doing my best to ignore television and newspapers. My lawyer warned me not to listen to or read about it. The news people aren't interested in the entire truth, only what will sell air time or papers. It's a shame, really."

"Yes, it is," Hailey said, unable to hold back. "Somehow, we have to demand to get the real stories out."

"The frustrating thing for me is I haven't been able to talk to Wallace about it. I don't know what his intentions were, why the money was divided like it was. There must have been some verbal agreements, some broken promises involved. Wallace wasn't always a pleasant man to be around, but he isn't the monster they're trying to make of him. I find it very suspicious for his partner to wait until after Wallace was placed in a nursing facility before making these claims."

"And now you have your home and life torn apart," said Hailey.

"I couldn't care less about the penthouse and most of the things in it. But to have my reputation marred like this is hurtful," Missy admitted. "I knew when I married Wallace that life wouldn't always be easy. Back then, some people were saying terrible things about the two of us being together because of the age difference. But those people didn't know Wallace like I did. He came from an unhappy background, and though he wanted and needed nice things around him, it was more about feeling accepted by others than it was about having things. They were a measure of success. Nothing more." Missy sighed. "I suppose we were alike that way. Now, I don't care. All I ever wanted was a family of my own. A happy one."

"And now you have one," said Hailey quietly.

Missy stared out the window and remained silent as tears filled her eyes.

To change the mood, Hailey said, "How is the painting coming along at the new house?"

Missy turned to her with a smile. "It's going well. I love the house already. Margaret knew what I was looking for, and you have excellent taste. And it's not far from here. I actually could walk here from it except for traffic on the road."

"I like that our houses are nearby," said Hailey. "All my relatives are in Idaho."

"That must be difficult for you," said Missy.

"Sometimes it bothers me," Hailey admitted. "But we talk often."

"It's nice that Janna is your friend. She's a lovely person, and I like Mike."

Hailey nodded. "Our families are close. We'll celebrate Thanksgiving here this year. We alternate."

"I'm looking forward to it," Missy said. "The girls and I are excited talking about helping you in the kitchen with pies and the stuffing. I always envied grandmothers who got to do that. Now I'll have the chance."

"They can hardly wait. You're very good with them."

"Thanks. I appreciate that. They make it easy. They're lovely children." She stood. "C'mon. Let me show you the progress on the house. I'll drive. It's practice for me after living in the city."

They went outside to the sleek black Mercedes Missy had occasionally used up north, climbed in and drove north on Gulf Drive, past the Salty Key Inn and into a tiny neighborhood clustered along the shore.

A truck sat in front of a two-story tan stucco house. "Great," said Missy. "They're still here. I want your opinion on something. You have exceptional color sense."

"I'd love to see it," said Hailey, pleased. Discussing details of the house with Missy had helped them grow closer. The house was six years old and had every convenience anyone could want, but the former owners had decorated with garish, bright wall colors that didn't work well together. The change in the interior with fresh paint was significant.

Hailey followed her inside and walked up the stairs to one of the rooms Missy had decided to use for an office. "We talked about a light pink for the walls, but I think it's not subtle enough. Tell me what you think."

Hailey stood at the doorway and peered inside. "I agree with you. It should be much lighter, so light you can't tell if it's pink or white."

"Thank you. I agree. Let me go talk to the painters. I'll be back. I want to show you some of the fabrics the decorator has shown me for valances over the blinds for this room and the downstairs master bedroom." She grinned. "I'm doing one of the rooms up here with the girls in mind hoping they'll want sleepovers here one day."

"They'll love it," said Hailey, feeling a pang of regret that her mother lived far away.

They were downstairs in the master suite when the doorbell rang.

Missy frowned and turned to her. "Would you mind getting that? I don't want anyone to know where I am."

"Sure," said Hailey. She walked to the front door and opened it, suddenly aware of a television camera being pointed at her. "What are you doing?" she asked, holding up a hand in front of her face.

"I'm sorry. I was looking for someone else. Guess I was wrong," the man said, lowering the camera from his shoulder. "I'm looking for Missy Linley. I was told she was somewhere in this area. Is she here?"

Hailey shook her head. "No, she isn't." Missy had already changed her name back to Missy Macklin.

The man shrugged. "Okay," he said agreeably.

She waited until he walked to his truck and got in before she closed the front door.

Missy came out of the bedroom. "I heard that. Someone in New York must have told them I was moving to Florida. Someone who knew exactly where." Her face fell. "It had to be the housekeeper. I wonder how much she was paid for that tidbit of information."

Hailey rushed over to her. "I'm sorry. That must hurt."

Missy drew a breath and nodded. "I'm not really the story, yet the press will make it impossible to escape. I think I'd better find another place to stay until my house is ready. I don't want to disturb the kids at your house."

The man from the television station was still outside, and Hailey suspected it wouldn't be long before others joined him.

Hailey drew herself up straight. "No. You have

every right to move to Florida, be with us. We can't let them take that away from you."

Missy let out a long breath and gave Hailey a grateful look. "Thank you. If you ever want me to leave your house, just say so."

Hailey shook her head. "That's not going to happen."

Two days later, Hailey was ready to change her mind. The same cameraman stood with a reporter at the end of her driveway. When she asked them to move, she was told they had the right to be there, and that particular portion of land was public.

Rolling her eyes, Hailey left them to go inside to call Brady's school to tell them she intended to pick up Brady instead of having him take the bus. She couldn't allow a nosy reporter to approach her children.

That afternoon as she drove past the reporter, she warned Brady never to speak to them, that they wanted information about Missy, and he was to say nothing.

He gave her a solemn look and nodded. "Missy doesn't like them. I know. She told me."

"We all like our own space from time to time. Right?" Hailey said.

Brady nodded.

"Well, this is a time when Missy needs hers. There's nothing to hide, really. She just needs her privacy."

"I need my privacy from the girls sometimes."

Hailey held in her laughter. "Yes, that's true. Now you understand why we won't talk to the reporters."

She'd had the same discussion with Luna and April. Though they couldn't appreciate the nuances of what she'd told them, they wanted to keep Missy happy.

Nick made it clear to the reporters they were not welcome, that no matter what they'd heard about Missy, privacy for his family is what was most important to them.

Still, Hailey was surprised by how her life had changed with reporters and others wanting information from her. She chauffeured the kids to keep them away from the press. She even gave up her morning walks to the Salty Key Inn and kept to the house. Their privacy wall in back of the house proved to be a blessing. But even with that protection, she felt as if she couldn't walk on the beach without someone tailing her.

At last, the trial in New York was settled out of court, ending some of the craziness. Though Missy was glad to have it over, had even encouraged giving Wallace's ex-partner what he wanted, the thought rankled Hailey. It turned out to be nothing more than a smear campaign and a disgusting money grab.

CHAPTER 11

Hailey awoke on Thanksgiving morning pleased for a normal day without reporters hanging around her house looking for a chance to talk to Missy. As intense as they'd been about trying to find a story, the reporters just as easily moved on to something else that held the promise of a different scoop.

It was a bright, sunny day, and plans for dinner moved ahead. As Nick had proudly told Missy, he was in charge of the turkey. Janna would bring a pecan pie, along with a vegetable casserole and a green salad. Hailey would make mashed potatoes, appetizers, and cranberry sauce.

Laughter erupted from the kitchen as the girls and Missy worked together on the stuffing, then the pies—both apple and pumpkin.

After morning chores were done, Hailey pulled Missy aside. "It's time to build sandcastles. It's a tradition that started when Brady first visited us. We continue to use sandcastles both for fun and for sorting out feelings."

"It sounds interesting," said Missy.

Brady and the girls stood by the back gate waiting for them. They each held a sand bucket and various small shovels.

Together they walked down to a spot on the beach where white sand was piled up.

"Looks like nature has done a lot of the work for us," said Hailey. "This will be perfect. Okay, kids, show Missy how we pack down wet sand in the buckets or make wet sand to use."

Hailey watched with satisfaction as all three children had a turn showing Missy what to do. Missy accepted all their instructions with a wide smile. Brady, especially, loved to tell her the proper technique of placing the buckets of sand together to form the building.

In time, they had the beginning of a large castle with several turrets. Luna showed Missy how to dribble wet sand on top of the turrets to make it look fancy. Then April handed small flags to Missy. "Now you can put those in. Be careful."

"I will," said Missy, placing them where she was told.

Hailey gave a last pat to a moat wall and knelt by the structure. "Now comes the best part. Placing people inside. Brady, why don't you start."

Kneeling beside her, Brady took a stick figure from a small net bag and placed it inside a small circle between the towers. "This is Daddy."

"I'm putting me in," said Luna, crawling forward

and placing another stick figure inside.

"Me, too," said April, copying her older sister.

"I'll place Brady inside," said Hailey.

"Mommy, this is you," said April, handing Hailey a stick figure.

"Okay," she said. "I'll place it inside. Now who are we missing?"

"Missy!" said Luna. "I've got one here." She carefully placed a stick figure next to the others.

"I've got Zeke and Tiger," said Brady, placing two more inside.

"I think we have everyone," said Hailey. "Right?" She waited for an answer. Sometimes other people were mentioned.

"It's all of us here," said Brady.

"Okay, then. What shall we wish for? We already have a lot to be thankful for." Hailey noticed the emotions racing across Missy's face and remained quiet.

"I wish every one of you here knew how thankful I am for you," Missy said quietly, giving each of them a long look. "I love you all."

It was quiet, then Luna said, "Is it okay if I wish for lots of presents for my birthday?"

Hailey laughed and exchanged amused glances with Missy. "Of course. You can wish for anything." Luna's birthday was in mid-December.

"I think I'd better wish for a better grade in math," said Brady seriously.

"Remember, we can make silent wishes too," said Hailey.

They sat in silence for a moment or two.

"Now is a good time to think of what you want to

say at the dinner table tonight when Uncle Mike asks us what we are thankful for," said Hailey. Sometimes the conversation turned heavy. She didn't want that to happen today for Missy's first sandcastle.

After a few minutes, Hailey stood. "How about a walk on the beach and then we'll go back and get ready for our company."

The kids took off at a run, leaving Missy and Hailey behind to pick up the shovels and buckets.

"Building sandcastles with the kids is a very sweet thing to do," commented Missy.

"It was a wonderful tool to use in helping Brady grieve for his parents. I thought he might include them in the castle today, but it's fine that he didn't. The option is always there for him or the other kids to intro-duce someone who's on their minds."

They strolled to the house in comfortable silence. After having to divulge many facts about herself and her marriage, Missy was usually pretty quiet, only occa-sionally offering tidbits of her former life. Hailey was fine with that. She herself wasn't a chatty person but spent a lot of her time thinking about her upcoming books.

Soon after they returned to the house, Janna, Mike, and their kids showed up. It was cute to see the bond Zoe and Brady had formed almost five years ago was still intact. After greeting each other, they took off for Brady's room to play video games.

Little Mikey was a handful, toddling about, checking everything out. Anxious to mother him, Luna trailed him, giving him instructions. April clung to Hailey until Missy offered to color with her, giving

Hailey and Janna time to talk while Nick and Mike discussed cooking the turkey.

"Let's take our iced tea out to the lanai," Hailey suggested. "It's been ages since we've had a chance to be together. You look fabulous, by the way."

Janna laughed. "I couldn't look worse, but I'm happy about it. We figure this little one will arrive around New Year's Day. Until then I'm going to look as if I've swallowed a watermelon."

Chuckling, Hailey put an arm around her as they walked out to the lanai.

"How are things going with Missy?" Janna asked her as she awkwardly settled in a chair.

"Great. The kids love having her here, and we've both been very careful about intruding on each other's space. Life sure has been full of surprises."

"For everyone," said Janna, patting her stomach. "Happy ones."

"Mike is extremely proud of you," said Hailey. "It's sweet to see."

"May I join you?" asked Missy, walking onto the lanai. "April decided she wanted to help Luna keep track of Mikey. Mike is watching them."

Janna patted the arm of the chair next to her. "Have a seat."

"Would you like some iced tea?" Hailey asked.

Missy shook her head. "No thanks. I wanted to give Mike and Nick a chance to talk." She sighed. "Mac would be about the same age as them, had he lived."

"Is being with us making you sad?" Hailey asked, concerned.

"No," Missy smiled, "being here with you is the best thing that's happened to me in a long time."

"I'm very glad it's all worked out. It's nice having you close by," Hailey said. "Especially now with Mom and my sisters so busy."

"But they're always a phone call away," said Janna.

"Oh, yes," Hailey admitted. "And I wouldn't want to leave Florida, except maybe on a hot, steamy summer day."

They laughed together. But Hailey's thoughts remained on her Idaho family. Four young women very different, but soul sisters forever.

CHAPTER 12

With memories of a pleasant Thanksgiving Day swimming in her mind, Hailey stood before boxes of Christmas decorations. She loved all the trimmings of Christmas—the lights, the carols, the Elf on the Shelf for the kids, and other traditions of celebrating the holiday.

Nick stood beside her. "I swear the boxes multiply in storage. Where are you going to put all these things?"

"I'm not sure." She pointed to a pile of separate boxes. "Those are your lights."

He groaned. "I might as well get it done. You and the kids will keep asking me for them if I don't."

She elbowed him playfully. "C'mon. You like Christmas as much as I do. I'll never forget my first Christmas with my mother and sisters. It was fabulous."

"You forget. My mother owned a candy store. Christmas meant working in the store helping her make candy."

"A dream job for any kid," she said, giving him a teasing smile.

"Not after a while," he said, laughing. "You're just trying to make me excited to put up the lights."

"True, but you like seeing them as much as I do. And the kids love them."

He nodded. "You're right."

Hailey smiled and lifted one of the Christmas boxes. She'd been pleasantly surprised to see how people in Florida decorated their homes, their landscaping, and her favorite, the trunks of their palm trees. Also, to her amusement, blow-up snowmen could be seen everywhere at this time of year.

"When is our tree going up?" Brady asked her.

"This evening, so Missy can do it with us before she moves out."

"I like having Missy for a grandmother," said Brady. "I love Grandma Maddie, but like she says, there's always room for more."

Hailey hugged him to her. "You're a very nice young man," she said. "And I love you." She planted playful smooches on his cheeks.

Laughing, he pulled away from her. "I know! Stop!"

She laughed with him, even as tears stung her eyes. She'd fallen in love with him when they'd first met at the library—a shy boy of four and a woman who knew what that felt like.

Luna and April joined them, and Hailey's attention was drawn to them. She recalled a book about two friends nicknamed Sugar and Spice. Those names suited her daughters too, with April all sweet and sugary and Luna a bit of an imp with spice. They made her laugh all the time.

That evening, Hailey observed the girls tugging on Missy's hand, leading her to the tree set up in the corner of the living room. She and Missy exchanged happy glances. It was obvious to Hailey that Missy loved all three children.

They were in the midst of decorating the tree when Missy received a phone call. She excused herself to take it. When she returned, her lips were trembling. "It's Wallace. He's gone. It happened unexpectedly. They think it was his heart." She shook her head sadly. "I should've been there."

Hailey went to Missy's side and wrapped her in a hug. "I'm sorry. But please don't blame yourself for not being there. Under the circumstances, I think he'd be glad you've done what was best for you."

"He'd be proud that while his ex-business partner managed to get a settlement, it was for less than he wanted," said Missy, thinning her lips in anger. "I'm thankful he never knew what was going on with that lawsuit. He would've been distraught if he knew about the betrayal, the way that vulture tried to scavenge money he wasn't owed."

"Yes, I'm sure you're right. Now, neither of you will have to worry about that," Hailey said in a soothing voice.

"I'll have to go to New York to settle some things."

She gave Hailey a pleading look. "Will you go with me?"

"Let me see what I can work out for babysitting with Nick and Taylor. When would we leave?"

"As soon as possible. I'll go, take care of things there, and make arrangements to have the two paintings I requested from the penthouse shipped to me."

"And maybe I'll meet with my agent," said Hailey. She'd been to New York for business several times, but didn't relish trips there. But she'd do this for Missy.

Even as they continued to decorate the tree, Hailey's thoughts remained on Missy and the upcoming trip. She'd been shocked at first to learn that many of Missy's friends had turned away from her when the lawsuit became public knowledge. She was even more surprised when those former friends made statements to the press and said horrible things about her. Others simply ghosted her.

Determination filled Hailey. She'd be there for Missy because others wouldn't.

Two days later, the kids lined up in front of the house with Nick waiting for her to leave. Missy had arranged for a driver to take them to Tampa to the airport. Though she'd be gone for only two nights, the girls and Brady were unhappy to see her leave.

Hailey gave them each a bear hug and a kiss, then turned to Nick.

"You've got everything you need?" he asked her.

She nodded. "I hope to be able to meet with my

agent and sign another contract while I'm gone, but mostly I'll be with Missy while she takes care of a few matters. We'll go to the facility in Connecticut where Wallace has spent these last few months and visit her lawyer in the city. That kind of thing. She has it all planned out."

"You're a good friend to her," Nick said, hugging her hard.

"I hope so. She's lost too many," Hailey said before placing her lips on his, making her wish she didn't have to go. She turned as a black limo drove up to the front of the house.

"It looks as if my ride is here. See you in a couple of days," said Hailey, suddenly feeling emotional about leaving.

"You'll be fine," Nick said, giving her one last kiss before carrying her suitcase to the driver who was standing by the open trunk of his car.

After giving them their privacy, Missy emerged from the house, rolling a suitcase behind her.

The kids surrounded her.

"'Bye, Missy. We'll miss you and Mommy," said Luna, throwing her arms around Missy's waist.

April and Brady moved in for hugs.

"Safe trip," said Nick, giving Missy a pat on the back. "We'll miss you."

"Thanks for everything, Nick. I really appreciate Hailey being able to go to New York with me. It makes it much more bearable."

"I'm glad you'll have someone to help you through this turn of events," Nick said solemnly.

He stood by with the kids as Hailey slid into the back seat of the car next to Missy.

Missy reached over and squeezed her hand. "Thanks for coming with me. I know it's hard for you to leave Nick and the kids behind."

Another time, Hailey might've tried to make light of it. But her relationship with Missy was deeper than that. She sighed. "You're right. But I wouldn't let you go alone to New York while some people there might give you a hard time."

"Thank you. I sometimes feels as if you're the daughter I never had." Missy pulled a tissue out of her handbag and dabbed at her eyes. "I'm an emotional mess. Everything has happened so fast."

"One step at a time," said Hailey, doing her best to offer encouragement.

At the airport, a sense of anticipation filled Hailey. Now that she was about to board the plane, she couldn't wait to see what awaited them in New York. Missy had promised a couple of fabulous dinners, and Hailey looked forward to that. New York was filled with a variety of excellent restaurants.

After they were settled in their seats aboard the plane, Missy turned to Hailey. "The way people whom I thought were my friends have treated me has brought back many unhappy memories of the abandonment I felt as a teen. I was a young woman who'd just given birth to a baby that she couldn't keep. I couldn't go home and really didn't want to.

So I had to make my way the best I could. Your very presence reminds me that I can survive anything."

"I'm glad," said Hailey meaning it. "I'm here to help anyway I can."

"I want to show everyone that Wallace and I aren't the horrible people they tried to portray. He stood by me in the past; now I'm doing the right thing by remaining loyal to him."

The midtown hotel where Missy had booked them was in a convenient location, close to MOMA and other tourist attractions. Hailey hoped she had the chance to visit the Museum of Modern Art. It was one of her favorite places to go when she was in the city.

After she got settled in her room, Hailey looked out the window at the activity below. New York was very intriguing, filled with a variety of people and their constant movement. Though she was normally content to stay home with her peaceful life, after being back in the city, she felt like putting on comfortable shoes and melting into the crowds to see what the excitement was all about.

At the sound of a knock at the door, she turned and hurried to answer it.

Missy smiled at her. "I thought you might like to see where I used to live. I need to talk to the doorman there. He's to let me inside to get the paintings that have been saved for me. Then he'll help me make arrangements for them to be picked up and shipped."

"I would love to see it. I was just thinking how nice a walk would feel."

Hailey bundled up in a warm coat, wrapped a scarf around her neck, and they took off.

Outside, it was sunny but cold.

They moved in silence as they set off at a brisk pace.

After they walked a few blocks north and a couple streets to the east, they stood in front of a tall building.

A doorman held open the door for them. "Good morning, Mrs. Linley. It's very nice to see you," he murmured as they entered the luxurious lobby.

Light-colored marble floors met columns of dark marble. Attractive seating arrangements of white plush furniture sat atop oriental rugs in front of fireplaces, inviting them to sit down. Beautiful gold-framed paintings were placed above the matching fireplaces on either side of the wide walkway through the space. Hailey's artistic eye took in every detail.

"Thank you, Jorge. It's nice to see you, too," Missy said, giving him a bright smile that did nothing to hide her emotions. "I need to go up to the penthouse to retrieve two paintings. They should be sitting by the door waiting for me. Then I must make arrangements through you to have them picked up and shipped to me."

Jorge tipped his head. "Of course. I'd be happy to help you." He sighed. "I was very sorry to see you go. You've always treated me with respect."

They studied each other for a moment before he led them to the elevator.

When the elevator stopped and opened at the top floor, Hailey stepped behind Missy into a small reception area in front of a wall with two oversized wooden doors leading to the penthouse. Resting against the wall were two large paintings.

"There they are," said Missy with satisfaction. She turned to Jorge. 'I'll call the gallery and set a time for them to pick these up. Then will you see that they get them?"

"Yes, of course." When Missy started to hand him some folded dollars, he held up his hand. "No, I'll do this for you because I want to. You've always been more than generous with me."

"Thank you," said Missy, tucking the money back into her purse. "I appreciate that more than you know."

Jorge shuffled his feet and looked up at her. "I know what some people did to you, and it's not right."

"No, it isn't. But as Wallace would say, 'that's life.'"

"He was sometimes a hard man, but a generous man too," Jorge said. "I will never forget what he did to help my family."

Missy smiled but said nothing as they turned to enter the elevator.

All the way down to the lobby Hailey thought of Jorge's words. They told more about Missy and Wallace than any official report could. She gazed at Missy, realizing there was a lot more to her than she'd realized. Wallace, too.

CHAPTER 13

Once they were on the street again, Missy turned to her. "It's time for tea. Does that sound tasty to you? It's too early for dinner."

"It sounds very elegant," Hailey said with a smile. At home, the kids would be restlessly waiting for Nick to get home.

Missy smiled with satisfaction. "There's a lovely little patisserie a short way from here. One of my favorite spots."

Le Croissant was in a small narrow space tucked between two larger storefronts. Inside, tables were covered in pink-linen cloths. Pots of pink silk flowers sat in the middle of the tables. The walls, painted a bold green, gave Hailey the added feeling of being in a garden.

They were seated at a table in the corner, giving Hailey the opportunity to see the customers who came in. Many appeared to be women who, like Missy, were in need of something light to eat before participating in a late dinner.

Missy's back was to the door so she was unaware when a middle-aged woman approached them.

"Is that you, Missy?" the woman said, causing Missy to startle in her chair.

Missy turned to the woman. "Eleanor, it's been a while."

"Oh, yes. I was sorry to learn that you've left the city. But then, with all that was going on, I understand." She stared at Hailey. "And who is this?"

Hailey paused, not knowing how to introduce herself.

"She's a trusted friend of mine," Missy said. "A blessing really."

"Oh, how nice," Eleanor said. "Well, time for me to go back home and get ready for dinner. The mayor and his wife are coming, along with some other people you know."

Hailey bit her tongue at the snide tone to the women's words. She wanted to protect Missy but had no idea what she could say.

Missy saved her the trouble. "I'm very happy to be out of that endless circle. Enjoy."

Eleanor gave Missy a surprised look then walked away.

"What was that all about?" Hailey asked.

Missy's nostrils flared. "Eleanor is one of those *dear* friends of mine who loved to spread gossip about me and Wallace once the trial started. She's just one. There were others too."

Hailey reached across the table and squeezed

Missy's hand. "I'm glad you don't have to put up with that in Florida."

Missy smiled. "Me, too. Now, let's enjoy something sweet along with a nice cup of hot tea. Tomorrow evening, we can walk over to Rockefeller Center to see the tree and the skaters, if you'd like."

Hailey smiled. "I would love that. I want to get pictures of the skaters to show the girls. At some point, we'll be going to Granite Ridge, and they can do some ice skating there."

At the hotel, Hailey went to her room while Missy took care of the details of going to Connecticut to sign papers and pick up the few belongings of Wallace's that she wanted to keep. The rest was going to charity.

The next morning, Hailey lay in bed, thinking of home. After a wonderful dinner at a Thai restaurant, Hailey had called home to talk with Nick. She'd talked to the kids earlier, but had missed her usual nightly conversations with Nick. As expected, he and Taylor were doing well handling the children. But talking to him wasn't the same as cuddling up next to him.

She got out of bed. After a shower and preparing for the day, she waited for room service to bring her breakfast. It was a luxury, especially in comparison to her usual hectic mornings.

Missy joined her after breakfast, dressed for the cold weather. "I've hired a limo to take us to the Evergreen Retreat. It's only an hour's drive, maybe a little more, but I'm anxious to get there and back. It's always been such a sad place for me."

"I understand," said Hailey, grabbing her coat.

As Missy had indicated, the drive was short. But Hailey noticed how tension in Missy grew as they got closer. She wondered what kind of relationship Missy had had with Wallace. There was definitely some tenderness there or she wouldn't be so loyal.

The retreat was really a hospital with a main building and a number of outlying buildings for those who needed special care. Set on rolling hills in the countryside, it was everything Hailey expected for an upscale facility of its kind.

The receptionist greeted them warmly, and within minutes, the director appeared in the lobby. He walked over to them and clasped Missy's hands in his own.

"Mrs. Linley, you have our deepest condolences. Wallace was an interesting patient who seemed to be holding his own. We'll have a complete report for you, but at the moment, it appears as if his heart simply gave out during the night. Come this way. We can talk and make final arrangements."

"Thank you," said Missy. "Fortunately, we were able to agree on what should be done in such an event before he was more or less lost to us."

"I'm going to wait here," said Hailey.

Missy nodded and followed the director down a hallway, leaving Hailey in the comfortable reception area, content to read a book on her phone.

Missy returned a short while later carrying a small canvas bag. "I'm ready to go."

"Okay," said Hailey jumping to her feet, noticing Missy's efforts not to cry.

They returned to the limousine, and once inside with the privacy window closed, Missy turned to Hailey. "A nurse told me that before he died, Wallace called her Missy and thanked her for everything." Tears overflowed from Missy's eyes and spilled down her cheeks. "For all our challenges, Wallace and I helped one another and remained true to each other. That's a strong lesson for me when many others turned away."

"I thought Eleanor was especially cruel. If I wasn't listening carefully, I might've thought she was being nice."

Missy nodded. "Polite veneers can hide a lot. I have an appointment with my lawyer this afternoon. May I treat you to a spa treatment?"

Hailey shook her head. "Thanks, anyway, but I'm going to wander into the MOMA. Then later, maybe do a little shopping. I'd hoped to see my agent but she's unexpectedly out of the office. But really, if you need anything, let me know."

"Thanks," said Missy. "Why don't I have the driver drop you off at the hotel? From there you can walk to the museum and over to Fifth Avenue. Let's meet back at the hotel here in time for cocktails and then go to dinner."

"That sounds like a plan," said Hailey, eager for some time on her own.

That evening as she headed down to the lobby bar to meet Missy, Hailey was very glad she'd chosen comfortable walking shoes for her afternoon. Now, wearing heels that would require cab rides, she felt better dressed.

Missy smiled and waved, rising from her chair at the small table where she was sitting.

Seeing her in this setting looking every bit a sophisticated New Yorker, Hailey smiled, proud to be with her.

Missy gave her a quick hug before Hailey sat down. "I can't tell you how happy I am that you've accompanied me. I had an awful run-in with a former friend outside my lawyer's office. Seeing your face has reminded me that I have a lot to look forward to."

"Of course. Remember, it'll soon be Christmas, and the kids have Christmas programs. There's nothing like seeing a child at Christmas to remind you of joy in the world."

Missy laughed. "Brady's already asked if I'm coming to the Christmas program. I assured him I was."

"It's wonderful that you get along with children. All three of mine are very excited about having you here. Nick and I are too."

"I remember how shocked you were when we first met," said Missy. "I don't blame you—a person from the past making such a claim. But after seeing the photograph of Brady, I couldn't let it go. Now, I'm glad I persisted. Life is such a balancing act dealing with the ups and downs."

"It seems almost mystical that you found us," said

Hailey. She'd thought about that a lot, marveling at the way people naturally come in and out of someone's life.

"Let's have a glass of wine and then head over to the Rockefeller Center. There, we can take both photos and videos of the ice skaters. With your permission, I'm thinking of giving the kids ice skates and lessons at a skating rink in Clearwater. What do you think?"

"It's a wonderful idea," said Hailey. "Just because we live where we do, ice skating shouldn't be off limits to them."

"Even April can ice skate, right?"

Thinking of her youngest, Hailey chuckled. "April can do anything she can put her mind to. At just four, she's able to keep up with Luna and Brady."

"She's precious," Missy said, as two glasses of red wine were placed on the table. "Hope you don't mind, but I've ordered pinot noir for us."

"Perfect," said Hailey. She didn't drink a lot but had learned the difference between an acceptable wine and one that wasn't. As they talked, conversation flowed easily between them, and Hailey suddenly realized they'd become friends.

The huge Christmas tree at Rockefeller Center was gorgeous. But what Hailey liked most was observing the number of people skating on the rink. It made her memories come alive. Living in Granite Ridge, Hailey and her sisters had all known an active outdoor life of ice skating, skiing, and playing in the snow. Hailey didn't think of it often, but now, pulling her coat closer, a pang of envy shivered through her.

They stayed a while and then moved to a Greek restaurant for dinner.

"This is what I'll miss most in New York," said Missy. "This ability to find different kinds of restaurants with tasty food from around the world, all within walking distance."

"It's unique," said Hailey. "But Miami isn't too far from us in Florida, and it being a tourist state, Florida is filled with lots of good restaurants."

"I know," said Missy, and for the first time on this visit, Hailey realized what a big change Missy was making.

CHAPTER 14

The next day when Hailey and Missy walked into the baggage claim area of Tampa International Airport and found Nick and the kids waiting for them, Hailey didn't know who was weepier—she or Missy.

Nick threw his arms around her and pulled her close before settling his lips on hers as if she'd been gone weeks not days. When they pulled apart, they smiled at one another.

"How was it?" Nick asked, glancing at Missy hugging and talking to the kids.

"Emotional, but nice," Hailey said. "I'm glad I agreed to accompany her. Later, I'll tell you about some of the people we met." She laughed as Brady, Luna, and April surrounded her, talking all at once as she hugged and kissed each one. With school out for Christmas vacation, they were bursting with energy.

With everyone and two bags loaded into the SUV, they headed home. After the hustle and bustle of the city, this area seemed very subdued. But it suited Hailey. As the saying goes "Home is Where the Heart is," and for her that was with Nick and the children.

As soon as Hailey got out of the car, she heard Zeke and Tiger howling and grinned to herself. Even those dogs made their house a home.

The dogs raced outside and ran in circles around them before Hailey and the others entered the house. She stood in the entry a moment and inhaled the scent of home. Being at home in her own house was precious to her.

Nick came up behind her and placed a hand on her shoulder. "We missed you," he whispered in her ear. "Me, most of all."

She turned and lifted her face to his. "In my heart, I take you and the kids with me wherever I go."

He kissed her then, long and deep, ignoring the kids making noise around them. She became lost in his embrace even as April tugged on her shirt.

"Ugh! Mushy stuff," groused Brady, bringing laughter out of Nick and Hailey, ending their kiss.

"Okay, kids, ready to surprise Mom and Missy?" Nick said. He took Hailey's arm and led her into the kitchen. "Welcome to Hensley's Italian Restaurant."

Hailey glanced at the table set for dinner, inhaled the garlic tomato sauce simmering on the stove, and clapped her hands. "For us?"

"We all helped," said Brady.

"I buttered the bread," April said proudly.

"And I made a salad with Dad," said Luna.

Hailey tried to hold back tears but finally couldn't

ignore her blurred vision. "This is so sweet. Thank you."

"Mom, don't cry," said Brady, giving her a worried look. "It should make you happy."

"Oh, but it does," she said. "I can't thank you enough. I don't know about you guys, but I want to build a sandcastle on the beach. Do we have time?"

A chorus of yeses came from the kids.

Together they walked out to the beach. After the chill of New York, the warmer temperature felt lovely on Hailey's skin. But the biggest warmth was inside her as she, Missy, and the kids worked together to build a sandcastle.

When it came time to place people inside, the five of them went first, then her mother and Missy, and as many relatives they could think of until there wasn't any more room.

"That's quite a crowd," Nick said.

Hailey smiled. "But remember the rule." She turned to Brady.

He grinned. "The rule is there's always room for more."

"Right," said Hailey, wrapping an arm around his shoulder. "Anyone hungry?"

"Beat you home," said Luna, taking off with Zeke and Tiger.

April followed her.

Brady walked with Missy.

Nick looked at Hailey. "Good to be home?"

"The best," she said, knowing she'd give up the glamour of a different life for this one anytime.

❄

With the trip to New York behind them, it was time for Missy to make the move to her own house. The thought both pleased and saddened Hailey. She'd become used to having morning coffee together before each started their separate days.

"I'll confess I'm going to miss being here," Missy said over coffee one morning. "But I have to begin a life of my own. Thanks to you and Janna, I have a part-time position at the library. That's a beginning. I've also looked into volunteering at the local hospital as well as working at one of the local hotels. We'll see."

"You have most of your furniture in place, but do you need to borrow anything from us?" Hailey asked.

Missy smiled and shook her head. "Thankfully, I've been able to start anew and will fill in as time goes by. Things are still being sorted out, but I should be fine in that department. My lawyer says now is the time to take care of it."

"I love that you've given the kids rooms at your house. They've become very attached to you, and knowing they have space with you makes the transition easier." Hailey smiled at Missy. "A few months ago, I would never have believed all this would happen to us. But as a friend once told me, you sometimes have to take a big leap forward and trust that things will go well. In this case, it couldn't be better." Hailey reached across the table and gave Missy's hand an affectionate squeeze. "We love you, Missy."

Missy gazed at her through watering eyes. "Today I can honestly say I think I'm in the right place at the right time. We can never leave our pasts completely behind, but we can build a better future from the ruins of it. I've kept my past hidden, but now it feels like a light that led me to you."

"What was done to you was a grave injustice, and I'm glad to see how things have worked out. I think Mac would be pleased to know how much you cared all these years and would admire your bravery in finding us."

Missy nodded. "I'd like to think so too.."

"The children will want to say goodbye to you this afternoon," said Hailey.

"I have an idea. Why don't you and the kids follow me to my house and I'll welcome them there?"

"Great idea. Let's do it." Hailey couldn't think of a sweeter arrangement.

That afternoon, Hailey and Missy made a game out of checking to make sure Missy's things were out of the guest room, giving each child something to carry to the new house.

Hailey and the kids drove behind Missy's car to her house and then waited for Missy to open the door to her house and wave them inside.

As they entered the house, they proudly handed Missy the item they carried.

Then Missy said, "Welcome to my new house. There's a special place for you, too. Better go check your rooms upstairs for when you come for a sleepover sometime."

"Is there a room for Mommy and Daddy too?" Luna asked.

Missy smiled. "Yes, there is. As your Grandma Maddie says …"

"There's always room for more," Brady finished.

The kids took off running upstairs.

Hailey and Missy stood in the front entry smiling at one another.

"Looks like a smooth transition," said Hailey. "Are you going to be okay?"

Missy smiled. "Better than ever."

December 23rd was a stormy day with a promise of a sunnier one. The kids stayed inside, reading and watching television, anxious for the time when they'd leave for the Christmas concert.

Hailey remained busy in her office. Because she hadn't been able to meet with her agent in New York, she'd sent in a few ideas for a new Charlie and Zeke book about meeting someone new and how families can come together. In the meantime, poor Henry, the rabbit who'd learned his lesson, was on his way home in the last pages of the book.

As she sketched samples for those pages, she thought about her stories. Many of them revolved around family. She knew why, of course. Thinking of Maddie, she called her and was forced to leave a message. Wishing her all kinds of love and promises to tell each of her sisters the same, Hailey ended the call.

Later, when it was time for Nick and Brady to head

to the civic center for the concert, Hailey gave them each a hug. "We'll be in the audience cheering you on."

She cupped Brady's face in her hands. "Are you okay? Not scared or anything?"

Brady shook his head. "I like singing. Like Dad."

She and Nick exchanged glances, then Nick said, "We'll see you later."

Hailey picked up Missy and they headed to the annual concert. People from all over the area attended it.

As they walked to the auditorium from the parking lot, Hailey was amused to see both of her daughters hanging onto Missy's hands. They loved the attention Missy gave them. Having her near had added even more excitement to the holidays.

Inside the auditorium where the Christmas concert was going to take place, the audience was growing.

Hailey and Missy guided Luna and April to their seats. The buzz of excitement added to Hailey's tension. It didn't matter how calm Nick and Brady were, her nerves were always on high alert before they performed. But then, due to shyness, it had taken years to admit that she was Lee Merriweather, the author of the beloved Charlie and Zeke books.

Sitting between her and Missy, the girls gazed around the area, occasionally waving to friends, waiting for the moment when the music would start. Nick and Brady were scheduled to begin the show by singing a Christmas carol Nick had adapted to guitar music and for a special solo to accommodate Brady's voice.

An announcer stepped onto to stage. "Good evening, ladies and gentlemen, girls and boys. Welcome to the tenth annual Christmas Eve Concert put on by the Chamber of Commerce. We have a wonderful evening of music for you. We will begin with a special duo—father and son, Nick and Brady Hensley. Sit back, relax, and welcome the holidays with this music.

The lights dimmed and the audience grew quiet as the curtains were pulled back. Sitting on a stool beside Brady, who was standing tall, Nick strummed his guitar. Then Brady's clear, pitch-perfect voice rang out with the beginning of *Joy to the World*, one of her favorite carols.

After the initial stanza, Nick's voice gently blended in with Brady's. A shiver ran through Hailey's body at the sound of them singing together. She thought back to that Christmas five years ago when she'd been given both a son and a daughter.

Tears blurred Hailey's vision.

Luna looked up at her with concern and nestled close. Missy reached over and patted Hailey's shoulder, sending a message of love. April got out of her chair and climbed up into Hailey's lap.

Rubbing April's back in soothing circles, Hailey continued to stare at the men in her life, mesmerized by their singing, the way father and son seemed right together. She felt Linnie's presence as she often did, and she wished she could thank her for the gifts of her children.

She looked down at April wearing glasses now and holding hands with Luna. This was how she and Alissa had been as children. They still were close.

Hailey's heart filled with joy at all she'd been given by one simple act all those years ago by a woman who'd opened her home to her. She caressed Luna's silky hair, grateful Luna had come into her life and heart. She, like Brady, was theirs because of their mother's loving thoughts for them.

Life had brought Hailey surprises, given her a childhood home, and later, a husband to love, and children of her own. Now, she had a second grandmother to her children, a woman who needed them as much as they loved her. She knew more surprises would happen, some good, some not. But they'd face them all together.

Joy could be measured by so many things, and, for Hailey, it was this moment with her special family. She'd hold it close to her forever.

CONTINUE THE STORY

I hope you enjoyed joining Hailey and Nick and their family for another Christmas. You won't want to miss the next book in the series – **Christmas Shelter by Tammy L. Grace**. Here are the links for it:

Amazon:
https://www.amazon.com/dp/B0B4HN5VDS
Books2Read:
https://books2read.com/
SoulSistersChristmasShelter

And if you haven't enjoyed the other Christmas stories in the series, here are the links for all of them.

1-Christmas Sisters - FREE
books2read.com/u/mdlxvw
2-Christmas Kisses by Judith Keim
books2read.com/u/mqr75v

3-Christmas Wishes by Tammy L. Grace
https://books2read.com/
soulsisterschristmaswishes

4-Christmas Hope by Violet Howe
https://books2read.com/ChristmasHope

5-Christmas Dreams by Ev Bishop
https://books2read.com/
ChristmasDreamsbyEvBishop

6-Christmas Rings by Tess Thompson
https://books2read.com/u/bwdaWY

7-Christmas Surprises by Tammy L. Grace
https://books2read.com/
soulsisterschristmassurprises

8-Christmas Yearnings by Ev Bishop
https://books2read.com/
ChristmasYearningsbyEvBishop

9-Christmas Peace by Violet Howe
https://books2read.com/sschristmaspeace/

10-Christmas Castles by Judith Keim
books2read.com/u/47NVOq

11-Christmas Star by Tess Thompson
https://books2read.com/ChristmasStarSoulSisters

12-Christmas Joy by Judith Keim
books2read.com/u/mqE5Mv

13-Christmas Shelter by Tammy Grace
https://books2read.com/
SoulSistersChristmasShelter

14-Christmas Secret by Violet Howe
https://books2read.com/SSChristmasSecret

15-Christmas Longings by Ev Bishop
https://books2read.com/
ChristmasLongingsByEvBishop

ACKNOWLEDGMENTS

Writing is a solitary business, so when friendships emerge with fellow writers, it's especially delightful. I'm so very pleased to call the other authors in this series friends— Ev Bishop, Tammy Grace, Violet Howe, and Tess Thompson.

I hope you enjoy these stories for the holidays and all year 'round. If so, be sure to share the news with your friends. And above all, have a wonderful joyful holiday season!

Finding Family – 4

The Salty Key Inn Series – Boxed Set

SEASHELL COTTAGE BOOKS:

A Christmas Star

Change of Heart

A Summer of Surprises

A Road Trip to Remember

The Beach Babes

THE DESERT SAGE INN SERIES

The Desert Flowers – Rose – 1

The Desert Flowers – Lily – 2

The Desert Flowers – Willow – 3

The Desert Flowers – Mistletoe & Holly – 4 (2022)

THE CHANDLER HILL INN SERIES

Going Home – 1

Coming Home – 2

Home at Last – 3

The Chandler Hill Inn Series – Boxed Set

SOUL SISTERS AT CEDAR MOUNTAIN LODGE

Christmas Sisters – Anthology

Christmas Kisses

Christmas Castles

Christmas Joy

Christmas Stories – Soul Sisters Anthology

OTHER BOOKS

The ABC's of Living With a Dachshund

Once Upon a Friendship – Anthology

Winning BIG – a little love story for all ages

Holiday Hopes

The Winning Tickets – (2023)

For more information: www.judithkeim.com

ABOUT THE AUTHOR

Judith Keim, a USA Today Best Selling Author, is a hybrid author who both has a publisher and self-publishes. Ms. Keim writes heart-warming novels about women who face unexpected challenges, meet them with strength, and find love and happiness along the way— stories with heart. Her best-selling books are based, in part, on many of the places she's lived or visited and on the interesting people she's met, creating believable characters and realistic settings her many loyal readers love.

She enjoyed her childhood and young-adult years in Elmira, New York, and now makes her home in Boise, Idaho, with her husband and their two dachshunds, Winston and Wally, and other members of her family.

While growing up, she was drawn to the idea of writing stories from a young age. Books were always present, being read, ready to go back to the library, or about to be discovered. All in her family shared information from the books in general conversation, giving them a wealth of knowledge and vivid imaginations.

Ms. Keim loves to hear from her readers and appreciates their enthusiasm for her stories.

"I hope you've enjoyed this book. If you have, please help other readers discover it by leaving a review on the site of your choice. And please check out my other books and series:

Hartwell Women Series
The Beach House Hotel Series
Fat Fridays Group
The Salty Key Inn Series
The Chandler Hill Inn Series
Seashell Cottage Books
The Desert Sage Inn Series
Soul Sisters at Cedar Mountain Lodge Series
The Sanderling Cove Inn Series
The Lilac Lake Inn Series

ALL THE BOOKS ARE NOW AVAILABLE IN AUDIO. So fun to have these characters come alive!"

Ms. Keim can be reached at www.judithkeim.com

And to like her author page on Facebook and keep up with the news, go to: http://bit.ly/2pZWDgA

To receive notices about new books, follow her on Book Bub:
https://www.bookbub.com/authors/judith-keim

And here's a link to where you can sign up for her periodic newsletter! http://bit.ly/2OQsb7s

She is also on Twitter @judithkeim, LinkedIn, and Goodreads. Come say hello!

Note: As part of her participation in the Soul Sisters at Cedar Mountain Lodge series, Ms. Keim is part of the Facebook Group: Soul Sisters Book Chat. To learn more about the five authors and to share friendship and fun with other readers, join here: https://facebook.com/groups/soulsistersbookchat